Refreshing Grace

By John P. Correia

Biblical Framework Press

ISBN-10: 0-9858958-0-2

ISBN-13: 978-0-9858958-0-8

I dedicate this book to my mentor and friend, Dr. Fred Chay, who taught me to think critically and understand all sides of an issue. It is Fred who has led me to try to think and teach fairly and in sincerity of understanding. For this I am forever grateful.

Acknowledgements

Of course, no project like this gets done without the help and encouragement of many. Any errors or deficiencies are of course fully mine, but any success is dependent upon people willing and able to help me. I am very grateful to Pastor Mark Martin at Calvary Community Church in Phoenix, AZ for hosting the seminar from which this book emerged and for his friendship and willingness to help me at every stage of the writing and production process. I am in debt to Dr. Roger Olson and Dr. Kenneth Keathley for encouraging me with their constructive and helpful feedback on different sections of the book.

Of course, writing a book takes a great amount of time and attention, and many gave me that time. I am grateful to my church family who supported me and encouraged me to spend the time necessary to write this book. I am grateful to Bryan Fergus for his editing skill and Josh Shoemaker for his input. Keith Krell, a friend who sticks closer than a brother, has been instrumental in helping me see the issues clearly. More than any others on earth, I am grateful to my wonderful children and of course my amazing wife Laura, without whom this book would never have happened. I am in so much debt for your generosity, Laura Marie, that it can never be repaid.

As always, any praise and glory belongs to God alone, for His greatness, goodness, and wisdom in all things.

Table of Contents

Chapter 1: Let's Have a (God-honoring) Fight!

There are a number of questions about salvation that cause more fights in church than we can shake a stick at. How does someone become a Christian? Does God choose people before time begins and then bring them to faith in Christ, or do people have free will and therefore responsibility to choose Christ for eternal life? Does God guarantee that all believers will persevere in a life of faith and good works, or is it our responsibility to keep the faith, which might not happen? What happens to a person who doesn't live a holy life or, after saying that they believe in Jesus, falls away and doesn't identify themselves as a Christian anymore? Were they never saved to begin with, or do they lose their justification[1]? Are they still saved while losing reward or blessing in time and eternity? Does God make salvation happen all on His own, or do we have a meaningful role to play?

---

[1] Within this book, the term "justification" is a legal term that refers to God *declaring* a person righteous by grace through faith in Jesus. A more technical definition is, "A forensic (legal) term related to the idea of acquittal, *justification* refers to the divine act whereby God makes humans, who are sinful and therefore worthy of condemnation, acceptable before a God who is holy and righteous. More appropriately described as "justification by grace through faith," this key doctrine of the Reformation asserts that a sinner is justified (pardoned from the punishment and condemnation of sin) and brought into relationship with God by faith in God's grace alone." It is taken from Stanley J. Grenz, David Guretzki, and Cherith Fee Nordling, *Pocket Dictionary of Theological Terms* (Downers Grove, IL: IVP Academic, 1999), 69.

These are big questions and they tend to generate a lot of heat but not much light. If you want to put someone on the defensive in a conservative, Bible-believing Christian church today, just ask them whether they are a Calvinist or an Arminian. It's worse than asking someone if they like Ford or Chevy, Coke or Pepsi, or if they're a Republican or Democrat[2]! The debate between Calvinism and Arminianism is almost as old as the Protestant Reformation itself, and both sides are firmly entrenched in how they see the issue. Worse yet, many Christians are somewhere in "no man's land" in between, not really Calvinist but not really Arminian. They might call themselves "Calminian," or if they're a theological hipster they might take the "holier than thou" road of saying that they don't like systems and are just "biblical."[3]

Even more, many Christians in church don't know where they stand on this issue and the debate scares them because it uses lots of big words and people fight about those big words a lot. And if theologians who do this for a living can't get it together, how can regular people hope to figure out what to believe? Unfortunately, we don't just get to dodge the issue. Jesus says that we each get to

---

[2] Unless there is a presidential election going on…then it's far more divisive to ask about politics!

[3] Of course, saying this is sure to start a fight because it implies the following attitude: "*I* am biblical, but you nasty heathen Calvinists and Arminians or Free Grace people are by definition therefore *unbiblical*. That might make me feel superior because I can claim the Scriptural high ground, but it's not going to make the discussion kind and certainly isn't playing nice!"

stand before God at the end of our lives and give an account of what we did with the gift He gave us.[4] While that evaluation might be primarily about our faithfulness to Him, we are certainly responsible for our understanding of God's character and called to love Him with our mind. (Matthew 22:37)

Each system of thought about salvation has points in its favor and points against it, and each has an easy memory device to help us remember them. Because of the memory device that each system uses to describe itself, the discussion can be likened to a flower bed.[5] Calvinists love their TULIP and defend it vigorously. Arminians are just as adamant that TULIPs smell bad and that they know God's goodness better; they prefer to plant LILACs in their garden. A system that is just gaining some renewed interest (though it is old) is Molinism; it describes itself with the acrostic ROSES and wants us to plant them in our garden instead.

What is the average person to do? Well, clearly the answer isn't to just roto-till the flower bed and allow crab grass to grow! And it doesn't seem best to decide what to "plant" in our salvation garden

---

[4] See the Parable of the Minas in Luke 19:11-27.
[5] I am by no means the first one to do this. At the very least, credit for the idea of comparing the three flowers belongs to Aaron Earls, "Theological Flower Bed: TULIP, DAISY & ROSES," *The Wardrobe Door*, August 2, 2010, http://wardrobedoor.blogspot.com/2010/08/theological-flower-bed-tulip-daisy.html. Online. (accessed June 13, 2012). His treatment of each is very brief, though, and doesn't explain each system with any depth.

before really taking the time to understand each system's flower and how it helps people understand salvation. Hopefully, at the very least, using flowers to describe and discuss each system makes it easier to remember them and hopefully makes for a friendlier conversation too. From a place of knowledge of each system with its strengths and weaknesses, we can make a more informed decision about which one seems to us to make best sense of the evidence of the biblical text. Since this issue generates a lot of emotion, though, let's begin by first laying down some rules to guide the discussion to come.

The First Rule: Play Nice!

One of Jesus' most famous commands, which we commonly call "The Golden Rule," comes in Luke 6:31, "And as you wish that others would do to you, do so to them." Our momma might have taught us this rule by simple saying, "Play nice!" Being mean-spirited, stubborn or pig-headed won't help one bit, whether we're talking about playing a game of checkers or discussing Christian theology. Let's never forget the wisdom of the proverb: "A soft answer turns away wrath, but a harsh word stirs up anger." (Proverbs 15:1)

It seems that in much of our theological dialogue we tend to "generate a lot of heat but not much light," as the old saying goes.

We have a lot of emotion attached to our view while many times we understand our way of seeing the Scripture only on the surface, and the other side at best casually or far more often not at all. Since our way is right and their way is wrong (in our mind at least), many times we never give them the time of day! Even worse, we accept what we hear about another's understanding without checking it with them and seeing if we have it correct from their point of view. It ends up looking like a big elementary-school playground war, with lots of insults and hurt feelings to match.

Rather than pitting ourselves against one another, it is far more valuable to realize that we all seek to serve the Lord who loves us. It's a whole lot nicer to work together, to dialogue and understand and consider than it is to throw insults at one another. It's worth it to take a moment to calm down, realize that this is a discussion that is an "in house" debate rather than defending the faith from infidels, and as the saying goes "take a chill pill." It's perfectly okay to be passionate about understanding God; it is not okay to be mean to others whose passion matches our own but whose understanding of the issue does not.

Now, that's not at all to say that the issue is not important or that it's not worth discussing; it certainly is, and it is absolutely worth talking about. We could go so far as to say that salvation is the most important topic in our lives to discuss! There are some important issues and distinctions between how Calvinists, Arminians, and Molinists understand salvation. These distinctions come from a fundamentally different starting place about what's first and foremost about God and about people, and lead to some different conclusions about how the Christian life begins, continues, and ends. These distinctions are important not only for theological discussions in a classroom or Bible study, but for how they impact the way we view the Christian life and how we live that life.

Even though the systems are different, it's important to understand that the differences are not so major that we are not talking with our brothers and sisters in Christ. In all of this discussion we must maintain a spirit of peacefulness and exhibit the attitude that Christ commands of His disciples in John 15:12, "This is my commandment, that you love one another as I have loved you." This is the heart behind our witness: that we seek to show love to one another and know what we believe the Scriptures teach, to have our distinctions clearly grasped, and to sharpen one another and always consider where we might be wrong in our own understanding of God and salvation.

It is helpful, then, when considering the systems of salvation within our camp of Christian theology to begin by remembering where we have the same ideas. Let's not forget that, while there

are some distinctions, there are a lot of similarities and a good bit
of agreement! Within this discussion, let's keep the following
areas of broad common understanding firmly in mind so that we
can frame the discussion in the Christian love and concern that
Jesus tells us we must have for one another:

1. **Scripture**: We are all committed to the inspiration,
   inerrancy, sufficiency, and authority of the 66 books of the
   Protestant Bible as our standard for faith and practice. We
   all believe that every part and every word of Scripture is
   the very Word of God without error in the original
   manuscripts.[6] It is the highest and final source from which
   we all take our understanding of every issue in the
   Christian life, this one no less than any other. We are all
   committed to obeying God as He has revealed Himself in
   Scripture and see the Bible as the final authority on every
   matter that it addresses. This certainly extends to the issue
   of our salvation! No one in this discussion thinks that the

---

[6] If you want to get geeky, we all hold to the Chicago Statement on Biblical
Inerrancy, which can be found at "The Chicago Statement on Biblical
Inerrancy" (International Council on Biblical Inerrancy, 1978),
http://library.dts.edu/Pages/TL/Special/ICBI_1.pdf (accessed June 21, 2012).
There's a short statement and a long statement with a whole bunch of
affirmations and denials, but for our purposes it means that God, without
overriding the personalities, background, styles and preferences of the human
authors of Scripture made sure that every word that was written in the original
manuscripts is the very Word of God. Further, it means that the manuscripts
that we have give us a reliable and accurate witness to those originals.

Bible is bunk; we're all reading from the same book and committed to being faithful to it.

2. **Christ**: We are all fully committed to the truth that Jesus is fully and completely God and fully and completely human, as well as to His Lordship and worthiness to receive all of our worship. Jesus Christ is fully God and fully human, and because of that He has "the name which is above every name." (Philippians 2:9) All within this discussion are passionate followers of Jesus and all desire to honor Him with their theology. No one here is trying to take Jesus off His throne or deny His full divinity or full humanity.[7]

3. **Trinity**: We all believe that God is one in Essence and three in Person, existing eternally as Father, Son, and Holy Spirit. We are all therefore "Trinitarian" in that we believe that God is Three in One, a Trinity. That's not to say that any of us can explain it with perfect understanding or grasp it completely, but we nevertheless all affirm that God is One in essence (Deut. 6:4) and yet the Father is God (Colossians 1:3), the Son is God (Colossians 2:9), and the Spirit is God (Acts 5:3-4) without the Father being the Son

---

[7] This is important to remember under the rule of "play nice." Many will say that their opponent's position subtly (or not-so-subtly) takes Jesus off His throne, or that another position lessens the sacrifice or glory of Christ in one way or another. However, each group fully affirms Christ in His divinity, humanity, and Lordship and to deny to them what they expressly affirm is dirty pool, which is certainly not playing nice!

or the Spirit, and the Son not being the Spirit. (Luke 3:21-22)[8]

4. **Salvation**: All three systems of salvation believe that human beings are saved by faith alone in Christ alone. In fact, the "five solas" of the Protestant Reformation[9] are all shared by all people in this discussion! Now there are certainly some in each camp who would point the finger at one (or more) of the other camps and say that they don't *really* believe that we are saved by faith *alone*, or don't understand what faith really is, but if you talk to responsible and thoughtful people in each camp they will all completely agree that we are saved by faith alone in Christ alone. We would all accept that the core of the gospel message is that Jesus, God Himself, became flesh and died for our sins upon the cross. He conquered death by rising from the dead and if we trust Him for eternal life we are saved. (1 Corinthians 15:3-8)

---

[8] It goes way beyond the scope of this book to discuss the subtleties of the Trinity; the point here is that the doctrine of the Trinity has been a test of Christian orthodoxy (i.e. a correct understanding of God) since at least the Council of Nicaea in 325 AD (and probably before that). We all hold it dear and it is a foundational point of agreement.

[9] They are: *Sola scriptura* (by Scripture alone); *sola fide* (by faith alone); *sola gratia* (by grace alone); *Solus Christus* (Christ alone); *soli Deo Gloria* (glory to God alone).

So let's be clear that each side in this debate has the "pillars" of historic, orthodox Christianity down pat. This is a discussion among Christians, not a witness to people of other faiths or no faith at all. Each system attempts to the best of its ability to describe what God says about salvation from Scripture. This can be an issue for passionate discussion, for disagreement, and for debate, but it should not be an issue for denunciation or damnation! We must never forget the maxim of the Reformation:

"In essentials, unity; in non-essentials, liberty; in all things, charity."[10]

This is how we present a godly witness to a lost and dying world; Jesus couldn't be clearer than John 13:35 about His first priority, "By this all people will know that you are my disciples, if you have love for one another." With this groundwork, it is acceptable and healthy to debate the systems and the passages vigorously and passionately to seek truth together. It is worthwhile to examine systems of belief! It can be very healthy to work through them

---

[10] This statement is often said to originate with the church father Augustine, though it never appears in his writings. It is instead most likely the work of a Lutheran theologian named Rupertus Meldenius; though he is not nearly so famous as Augustine, his words are nevertheless important to follow! For more, see Mark Ross, "In Essentials Unity, In Non-Essentials Liberty, In All Things Charity," *Ligonier.org*, September 1, 2009, http://www.ligonier.org/learn/articles/essentials-unity-non-essentials-liberty-all-things/ (accessed July 4, 2012).

together to seek answers as to which ones answer more of the questions of Scripture and which among the options holds the fewest problems. Let's never forget, though, that these kinds of endeavors are not helpful to the cause of Christ if they are handled in a condemning or angry manner. Imagine what it must look like to non-Christians that Christians are yelling at one another over these things.

So the first rule we should all follow all the time in this discussion is an important one: play nice! Jesus tells us in Luke 6:31 that we should treat others the way that we want to be treated, and certainly we would prefer that other Christians not call us heretics because our understanding of how a person comes to faith alone in Christ alone is slightly different than theirs[11]. That means that we have to obey Jesus by not calling them a heretic, and be kind and thoughtful in the discussion of systems of salvation. We need to appreciate and value the flowers others have planted in their gardens if we expect them to appreciate ours. To put it another way, we can all use some Refreshing Grace from one another!

---

[11] This is quite different than discussing with someone who says that people are not saved by faith alone in Christ alone. Someone who says that we must have good works to go to heaven or that there are other paths to God but Christ are not part of this discussion because they are not part of historic, orthodox Christianity. Even there, though, we should certainly play nice too.

The Second Rule: Seek to Understand Before You Disagree

We tend to have a terrible habit of entrenching in our positions without really considering alternatives; when we do this, it becomes like World War I trench warfare. The stalemates of that terrible war[12] are eerily similar to the stalemates regarding the debate around salvation, but as the famous saying goes, "It is the mark of an educated mind to be able to entertain a thought without accepting it."[13] In other words, to be educated and mature we need to be willing to see the issue (whether politics, parenting, or predestination) from the other side and consider the strengths and weaknesses of those with whom we disagree. In this vein, we must be sure to listen to the warning of Arminian theologian, speaker, and writer Roger Olson, who states:

> One principle that ought to be observed by all
> parties to this debate is *Before you disagree make*
> *sure you understand.* In other words, we must
> make sure that we can describe another's

---

[12] It really was terrible stuff. See John Ellis, *Eye-Deep in Hell: Trench Warfare in World War I* (Baltimore, MD: The Johns Hopkins University Press, 1989).
[13] This quote is often attributed to Aristotle, though it is not found in any of his writings, at least in this form. For some research on this, see "Denouement: Aristotle and accuracy," *Denouement*, February 22, 2009, http://publicnoises.blogspot.com/2009/02/aristotle-and-accuracy.html (accessed June 12, 2012).

theological position as he or she would describe it
before we criticize or condemn.[14]

Unfortunately there is not enough of this going on in the
evangelical Christian world today. It seems that we'd prefer to
hurl rocks at one another from our side of the debate rather than
listen to find the real distinctions so that we know where we
disagree. It's almost like we're the Hatfields and McCoys, less sure
of why we're fighting but positive that the other side is wrong and
needs to be punished. But if we do it right, listening to all sides of
this debate can deepen our walk with Christ, help us understand
Him better, and even build relationships with other Christians.

The way to have a truly meaningful debate is to engage and
dialogue, and that is the aim of the rest of this book. To truly
decide for ourselves which understanding of how a person comes
to faith alone in Christ alone takes the biblical witness most
consistently, we must first try to honestly understand how each
side sees the evidence and describes the process.[15] We must look
at them from their own point of view to try to get away from the
caricatures that are so common, because they do the discussion no
good. We must try to think and analyze each position for its

---

[14] Roger E. Olson, *Arminian Theology: Myths and Realities*, Fifth Printing.
(Downers Grove, IL: IVP Academic, 2006), 41.
[15] I am not arguing here that justification is a process (that would be quite
Catholic and not at all evangelical Protestant!), but using the term to describe
how the systems see the "event" as a series of arguments and/or logical steps.

strengths and weaknesses (each system has both!) so that we cannot only decide which one is most faithful to the biblical text but so that we can also thoughtfully interact with our friends, family, and fellow Christians about salvation, sovereignty, self-will, and systems of thought.

Each system in this discussion has been organized with a memory device known as an acrostic, with each having a flower associated with its position. Though there are limits to the value of these memory devices, they nevertheless can help us to understand and bring to mind the fundamental ideas of each system and keep them clear. Calvinism cultivates TULIP, Arminianism grows LILAC[16], and Molinists come up ROSES.

Acrostics like these are memory devices to give us a catchy way to remember things. Memory devices like this are common and they're helpful; many of us remember ROY G. BIV for the colors of the rainbow (Red, Orange, Yellow, Green, Blue, Indigo, Violet). Everyone knows what SCUBA gear does.[17] In math, many of us learned "Please Excuse My Dear Aunt Sally" as a reminder for the order of operations. (Remember? Parentheses, Exponents,

---

[16] DAISY is more commonly associated with Arminianism, but it is often used by Calvinist writers as a caricature of Arminianism or to use terms that aren't helpful to the discussion. LILAC is less commonly known, describes the system well (as we shall see), and avoids the caricature.

[17] Did you even remember that it is an acrostic? It is...Self Contained Underwater Breathing Apparatus.

Multiplication, Division, Addition, Subtraction). There are many more, showing that acrostics are helpful tools in our everyday life to help us remember concepts that can get complicated to remember without them.

These tools will help us understand, and that's our job. We can't really decide which system we think is best if we don't really understand what each acrostic means and how each system of salvation works. We must seek to understand before we disagree.

The Third Rule: Be Noble Bereans

Our third rule as we begin this study should characterize every discussion we ever have and every topic we ever study. We must search the Scriptures for ourselves rather than accepting even what an authority says without examination. We see a great example of this in Paul's ministry. In Acts 17 Paul and Silas are basically chased from Thessalonica because they stirred up the Jews there. In 17:10-11 Luke tells us about their reception in neighboring Berea: "The brothers immediately sent Paul and Silas away by night to Berea, and when they arrived they went into the Jewish synagogue. Now these Jews were more noble than those in Thessalonica; they received the word with all eagerness, examining the Scriptures daily to see if these things were so." The Bereans listened to Paul and Silas but they didn't just buy what they said whole cloth; instead, they searched the Scriptures[18] diligently to see if what Paul said squared with what the Bible said.

That is our task as well, and one we should relish! When diving into this issue (or any other) we should read the book in question or listen to the sermon or speech with a pen in one hand and a Bible nearby, ready at all times to look up a reference. With a book (like this one!) the pen lets us write thoughts in the margins, underline important statements, and makes us read actively. The Bible lets us check Scripture references and read the paragraph and chapter they occur in to get their context, as well as observe them carefully. In this manner we too can be "noble Bereans" as we pursue the issue of salvation and systems, asking whether we should plant our theological garden with TULIPs, LILACs, or ROSES.

I would encourage you, then, to get a pen or pencil, a highlighter, and a Bible before you read further.[19] Use them each liberally as you read. Look up references, pray as you go and look at each idea carefully to see if it has merit in light of the text of the Bible. If

---

[18] Remember, Luke (the author of the book of Acts) is not talking about the New Testament here; Paul and the other New Testament writers hadn't written it yet! Instead, "the Scriptures" in this verse is a reference to *their* Scriptures, i.e. what we would call the Old Testament.

[19] The classic book to learn more about how to read a book well is Mortimer J. Adler and Charles Van Doren, *How to Read a Book: The Classic Guide to Intelligent Reading* (New York: Simon & Schuster, 1972). It's worth your time to read!

you come to a word you don't know in the book, stop a second and either grab a dictionary like *The Pocket Dictionary of Theological Terms* cited earlier or get your Google-Fu working to look it up before moving on.

Now the task begins in earnest. We have our three rules (play fair; seek understanding before you disagree; be a noble Berean) and the task set before us. So let's get to examining our flowers! Our goal is to find out which species of flower we should plant in our garden: TULIPs, LILACs, or ROSES.

Questions for Individual Thought and Group Discussion:

1. Which of the three rules is hardest for you to apply? Why do you think that is?

2. Do you think it is possible for Christians to "major in the majors" in issues like this, or must we agree completely in order to get along?

3. If we hold to one system and have friends who believe differently (within the "four pillars" above), can we be friends and worship together or should we go our separate ways?

4. Honestly before God, are you willing to change what you think about Him and how He works, or is your mind made up?

5. If this is an issue that we don't have to completely agree on, why is it worth discussing at all? What is the value of investigating issues that are secondary in Christian theology?

Chapter 2: Calvinism- Cultivating TULIPs

Our first flower gets considered first because of its prominence in the American evangelical Christian world today. As we will see, Calvinism likes a pretty flower: TULIP! The TULIP will remind us of how Calvinism understands God's work in bringing someone from their natural state to enjoying God forever. That's a big task to ask of a flower.

It will be helpful in remembering which system teaches what to think about how the flowers of each garden are planted. In Calvinism, God and *only* God plants the TULIP in the garden of salvation. Keep that in mind as we look through the system: God does ALL the work from start to finish[1] in planting a TULIP in the garden. It's God's flowerbox, and if TULIPs are planted it is because God planted them.

Though the acrostic TULIP is helpful, we can't forget that not everyone understands it in exactly the same way. When discussing any system of theology it is sometimes difficult to represent every person who holds that system. This is no less the case in talking about Calvinism than in anything else. Five hundred years after it

---

[1] To use the big theological word, in Calvinism salvation is monergistic. The term is from the Greek words *mono* (meaning one) and *ergos* (meaning work). God is the one doing all the work!

was first described by its patriarch, John Calvin, Calvinism has grown and evolved with its continued use and discussion.[2] It might even be appropriate to discuss *Calvinisms* rather than thinking that the system is completely uniform. It's not, and there are people who hold to varying degrees of the different aspects of Calvinism along a spectrum. There are a lot of varieties of TULIPs out there, so to speak. There are Scottish Calvinists, 4-point Calvinists, New Calvinists, and the list goes on and on. It's important to keep in mind when talking to someone who says that they are a Calvinist that they might have some understandings that don't 100% line up with classic Calvinism.

In fact, many people use the term "Reformed Theology" as a synonym for Calvinism, and having multiple terms to describe a system can be confusing to people trying to study it.[3] We will refer to the system as Calvinism because it works as well as calling it "Reformed Theology" and at the same time pays tribute to its founder and chief proponent. For the most part, the terms are interchangeable and using the term "Calvinism" is easier for our purposes.

---

[2] For a great discussion of the development of Calvinism from the writings of Calvin to the Westminster Confession, please see R. T. Kendall, *Calvin and English Calvinism to 1649* (Eugene, OR; Wipf & Stock Publishers, 2011).
[3] We will see that Arminianism and Molinism also have multiple names that they are known by, so this is not a problem just within Calvinism and makes the discussion more confusing. Who said theologians make sense?

This system is accepted by some of the most notable evangelical Christian writers and speakers in America today. Well-known pastors such as John Piper, Mark Driscoll, Francis Chan and John MacArthur are Calvinists in their understanding of salvation.[4] Theologians and writers like Wayne Grudem, D.A. Carson, Mark Dever, R.C. Sproul, and Al Mohler are all within the Calvinist tradition. There are certainly more, but these are proponents known to many and represent the most popular understanding of the system known as Calvinism in America today.

Though there is theological diversity in some aspects of the system, Calvinism is known specifically for its understanding of how God accomplishes salvation in the life of believers. Within the popular speakers and writers who identify themselves as Calvinist there is sometimes disagreement as to *exactly* how the system works or how to express the doctrines; they all like particular types of TULIPs. Even though there may be different shades, at the end of the day a TULIP is a TULIP, and within Calvinism there is a long-held standard of discussion when it comes to understanding how the Bible describes salvation. Known as "High Calvinism"

---

[4] They all have unique approaches to the system, but at the end of the day their writings and speaking all point back to the Calvinist idea of TULIP with regards to salvation. Again, that is not to say that they all agree on every tiny point, but that they are in broad agreement under the tent of Calvinism.

or, for the academic, "Dortian Calvinism"[5], all Calvinists line up behind the acrostic TULIP as a handy way to understand how God takes a sinner and brings them from their natural state of sinfulness to enjoy the blessings of salvation for all time. This memory device stands for <u>T</u>otal depravity, <u>U</u>nconditional election, <u>L</u>imited atonement, <u>I</u>rresistible grace, and <u>P</u>erseverance of the saints.

The acrostic TULIP is a way to describe how Calvinism understands God's work in accomplishing the salvation of the saints. Because of that it is a helpful device to use to describe Calvinism as a system describing and explaining salvation, as well as a tool to help us remember its distinctives. When thinking "what would a Calvinist say about this issue or this passage?", we can remember Calvinism's flower and use the acrostic TULIP to locate the part of the system that addresses the issue we are considering and from that grasp how Calvinism understands a particular point or passage of Scripture. This will hold true for the other systems as well, as we shall see. For instance, while reading Hebrews 6:4-8 we might ask how a Calvinist would understand it, and realize that the P in TULIP stands for Perseverance of the Saints. Since these people didn't persevere in the faith but fell away according to v. 6,

---

[5] The name comes from the Synod of Dort (or Dordt) in 1618-19, where the Canons of Dort were adopted that are the five points that will be described in this book. To read the Canons of Dort, visit "The Canons of Dordt", n.d., http://www.reformed.org/documents/canons_of_dordt.html (accessed June 12, 2012).

a Calvinist would say that they were never really saved to begin with.

The system of Calvinism described by TULIP works its way from start to finish through the letters of the flower. It's a step-by-step understanding of how God accomplishes His goals in salvation, which can help us to remember it. It all starts with Total Depravity, which we will look into shortly. Total depravity logically leads to the concept of unconditional election; unconditional election is the grounds for limited atonement; limited atonement sets the logical need for irresistible grace; irresistible grace is a prerequisite for and logical reasoning behind the perseverance of the saints. It's a lot like a train, with each subsequent car being pulled by the one in front of it and being driven by the engine.

These all need explaining for sure, but remember that one leads to the next. Some Calvinists even like to add an S for the Sovereignty[6] of God to the acrostic to make sure that we don't forget it in the equation too![7] Therefore we must study the system

---

[6] Sovereignty is "[t]he biblical concept of God's kingly, supreme rule and legal authority over the entire universe." Grenz, Guretzki, and Nordling, *Pocket Dictionary of Theological Terms*, 109.

[7] Funny enough, even though TULIPS would work well, I know several Calvinist friends who prefer to put it first because the system does proceed first and foremost from the sovereignty of God. However, STULIP is not a pretty flower and is not easy to remember, so let's go with TULIPs (making the S small because not all include it in the system) for the sake of our garden analogy.

from start to finish in order to see how it describes the process of God bringing people to experience the blessings of salvation.[8]

In our look at Calvinism it is also good to think about the "center" of the system. Each of the systems of salvation that we will look at has a picture of God at its center, and that picture of God influences how the system describes God's ways. In Calvinism, God's greatness is at the center of everything. His majesty, sovereignty, and control over all events are what make God worthy of our worship to Calvinists. God's kingly majesty and absolute authority over every detail of creation is, in their understanding, the very heart of Scripture and a requirement for God's dealings with us to be grace-based.

Now knowing the center of the system and the big picture of how Calvinism proceeds, let's dig into each letter in TULIP to understand how it describes salvation from start to finish.

---

[8] The description of these points can be found in numerous Reformed writers, but is taken here from several of the ablest and most popular proponents of the system. Wayne Grudem, in his book, *Systematic Theology: An Introduction to Biblical Doctrine* (Grand Rapids, MI; Zondervan, 1994), sets the standard that theology students in many Calvinistic seminaries, Bible colleges, and Sunday School classes use in studying Calvinism. More support that this is a consistent view of modern Calvinism is drawn from David N. Steele, Curtis C. Thomas, and S. Lance Quinn, *The Five Points of Calvinism: Defined, Defended, and Documented*, 2nd ed. (Phillipsburg, NJ: P & R Publishing, 2004). Steele, Thomas, and Quinn have done a good job of putting together a readable understanding of the five points which is helpful to new readers. Finally, Michael Horton's *For Calvinism* (Grand Rapids, MI: Zondervan, 2011) is a great resource on classic Calvinism and the arguments for it.

Total Depravity (or Total Inability)[9]

Depravity means humans are bad…very bad. We are depraved in our nature and our situation is grim: "*Depravity* refers both to the damaged relationship between God and humans and to the corruption of human nature such that there is within every human an ongoing tendency toward sin."[10] Our natures are corrupt because of the Fall, and that corruption means we have a bent toward sin. An ongoing tendency toward sin would be one thing, but the reality is that "every part of our being is affected by sin—our intellects, our emotions and desires, our hearts…our goals and motives, and even our physical bodies."[11]

Calvinism says that humanity is completely and totally depraved. *Total depravity* means that we have no ability (and no desire even if we had the ability) to do anything that will in any way please God; humans cannot initiate anything in salvation because we are "dead in our trespasses and sins." (Ephesians 2:5) We are so alienated that nothing we do is pure or absolutely noble, and nothing in us would ever genuinely seek to honor God.

---

[9] Grudem, *Systematic Theology*, 497–498; Steele, Thomas, and Quinn, *The Five Points of Calvinism*, 18–26; Horton, *For Calvinism*, 35–52.
[10] Grenz, Guretzki, and Nordling, *Pocket Dictionary of Theological Terms*, 37.
[11] Grudem, *Systematic Theology*, 497.

This is not to say that we never do anything good before becoming Christians or can't ever seek anything we would describe as good; of course, there are plenty of examples of unbelievers doing morally good things and being good people in some sense. What the doctrine of total depravity *does* say is that any good that we do is tainted, earns no favor with God, and is not admirable in God's eyes. Our depravity taints everything like a drop of poison taints a glass of water; even if most of it is good, the part that is bad spreads into everything and renders it worthless. Total depravity says that *spiritually* we cannot do anything of any value or worth in the eyes of God because we are so totally messed up in nature and desire that our every action, even religious effort or attempt to please God, is tainted by sin and is therefore worth nothing in God's eyes. Our good looks to God a lot like a cat bringing its owner a dead bird it has caught. While the cat thinks it has done something nice, to the owner it's gross!

Within Calvinism's understanding, sin has so tainted our nature and our desires that we would never seek God on our own. Scripture says that unbelievers are "dead" (Ephesians 2:1; Romans 11:15; Colossians 2:13; James 2:17) and that description is the reason that depravity is called "total." We're not *mostly* dead; we're all dead in our trespasses and sins.[12]

Yes there are plenty of religious people out there who are trying to make God happy with their efforts, but even this argues for total depravity in the minds of Calvinists because those efforts are tainted by self-interest and empty of the grace of God. (Romans 2:17-24) They are works of self-righteousness that are not only worthless, but actually are contemptible to God. (Galatians 3:10) Our best efforts add up to nothing because a spiritual corpse can't accomplish anything. It's dead.

Just as a corpse can't do anything to make itself alive,[13] unbelievers have no hope of doing anything on their own that would bring them any merit in God's eyes. It is only the power of God that could possibly bring a corpse to life. Calvinism, then, begins with the premise that humanity is totally and utterly depraved, completely unwilling and unable to come to God unless God works a supernatural renewal in the heart of a person to bring them to life.

Calvinists point to several Scripture verses that speak to this point in especially clear or emphatic terms:

[12] If you read that in the voice of Miracle Max from "The Princess Bride," you're a true nerd.
[13] I think we've all had about enough of the fixation on zombies in our culture, so let's not go there.

- Isaiah 64:6: "*We have all become like one who is unclean, and all our righteous deeds are like a polluted garment. We all fade like a leaf, and our iniquities, like the wind, take us away.*" In this verse Isaiah points to all of the people around him and laments their hard hearts. More to the point, the best righteousness that anyone has is detestable before God; our best works are a "polluted garment." This speaks of the depth of the depravity of all people, because if Isaiah could look at Israel, God's chosen people, and say this then surely it would be no better for any Gentile!

- 1 Corinthians 2:14: "*The natural person does not accept the things of the Spirit of God, for they are folly to him, and he is not able to understand them because they are spiritually discerned.*" Paul in the context of this verse contrasts those who do not know Christ with those who do. The "natural person," or in other words the one in their natural depraved state of unbelief, has no ability to understand or accept the things of God. In our natural state, unbelieving people hold God in contempt and His word is ridiculous. There is no motivation, inclination, or capacity to seek God for those who are not God's. We don't seek God on our own; in fact we actively reject Him.

- Romans 3:10-11: "*None is righteous, no, not one; no one understands; no one seeks for God.*" (a quote of Psalm

14:1,3) This verse is part of the climax of the depravity of all people in Romans. Paul is wrapping up his section on the total sinfulness of humans from 1:18-3:21 and here he quotes the Psalms to reinforce to his reader that no one, in their own power, seeks after God. Likewise, no one is righteous. All of humanity is utterly and totally depraved.

- John 6:44: *"No one can come to me unless the Father who sent me draws him."* In this verse Jesus addresses some Jews who grumbled about Jesus' claim to have come from heaven (6:41). In response, Jesus tells them that He is not surprised that they are upset at Him, because only those who are drawn to Him by the Father come to Him. This speaks to total depravity within Calvinism because without the drawing of the Father no one would come to Jesus. The reason that no one would come to the Jesus unless the Father draws them is because they are totally and utterly depraved.

Unconditional Election[14]

Because we are all totally depraved, nothing we could ever do would earn anything from God. Even more, the doctrine of total depravity means that we would never seek God on our own. (Romans 3:10-11) Therefore, for anyone to be saved requires God to step in and save them actively and completely. And that means that God must first decide who He wants to save! Total depravity leads to unconditional election.

Unconditional election is the next step in the Calvinist system. God decides completely of His own choice, with His reasons, and for His glory who will be saved without any merit or reason on their part. "Election is an act of God before creation in which he chooses some people to be saved, not on account of any foreseen merit in them, but only because of his sovereign good pleasure."[15] Since we are all in the same boat of total depravity, it certainly can't be because some of us are good enough for God to choose us

---

[14] Grudem, *Systematic Theology*, 669–684; Steele, Thomas, and Quinn, *The Five Points of Calvinism*, 27–38; Horton, *For Calvinism*, 53–79. This is a major topic in Calvinist thinking, and there is a lot written on the topic. For more on this in particular from a Calvinist perspective, please see Sam Storms, *Chosen for Life: The Case for Divine Election* (Wheaton, IL: Crossway, 2007), R. C. Sproul, *Chosen by God* (Carol Stream, IL: Tyndale House Publishers, Inc., 1994), or John Piper, *The Justification of God: An Exegetical and Theological Study of Romans 9:1-23*, 2nd ed. (Grand Rapids, MI: Baker Academic, 1993).
[15] Grudem, *Systematic Theology*, 670.

and others aren't. God doesn't look at a graveyard full of corpses and pick the pretty ones!

This electing action of God is known as *unconditional* because it is not based upon anything that God sees in someone (including faith on their part); there is nothing in any person that merits God choosing them. (John 1:13) Instead it is simply His good pleasure to save some people out of the total number of depraved humanity. This, within Calvinism, is a cause for rejoicing in the grace of God. It is not an injustice that God chooses some over others; instead, election is a reason to rejoice, just as it is cause to rejoice when an emergency crew can save some people out of a burning building. God could absolutely have left all of us in our sin and total depravity, justly condemning us all because our own choices took us away from Him. Instead, because of His grace and mercy and for His good pleasure He chooses to save some, and that is cause for celebration.

To Calvinists, if God sees anything in someone (including their trusting Christ) as the reason that He elects them, this would be at least the beginning of salvation by works. We would receive at least some credit because there would be something praiseworthy or good that we have done that causes God to choose us. Only God should get the glory in salvation. (Revelation 4:11) Therefore election is seen as completely and totally the act of God in which

He takes all of the action to choose some people out of the total of depraved humanity and bring them to Himself. Only then is salvation truly all of grace and truly all for the glory of God.

There are several Scripture verses that, to Calvinists, point to the idea of Unconditional Election in no uncertain terms:

- Acts 13:48: "*And when the Gentiles heard this, they began rejoicing and glorifying the word of the Lord, and as many as were appointed to eternal life believed.*" This verse tells us that the ones who believe are those who are appointed to eternal life. The implication of the text is that those who believe, do so because they were appointed and not the other way around. Therefore election is unconditional because God elects without taking any foreseen faith into account on the part of the person. Because God elected them, they believed and were saved.

- Ephesians 1:3–5: "*Blessed be the God and Father of our Lord Jesus Christ, who has blessed us in Christ with every spiritual blessing in the heavenly places, even as he chose us in him before the foundation of the world, that we should be holy and blameless before him. In love he predestined us for adoption as sons through Jesus Christ, according to the purpose of his will...*" Paul's great treatise on election starts with these three verses (and continues until verse 14). In it, he says that God "chose us in Him." This occurred "before the foundation of the world," and has no conditions on our part attached to it. Because He elected us He decided our destiny in advance for us to become His sons through faith in Christ; in other words, election causes predestination. The whole package says that God elects without any merit or foreseen faith on the part of people.

- Romans 8:28–30: *"And we know that for those who love God all things work together for good, for those who are called according to his purpose. For those whom he foreknew he also predestined to be conformed to the image of his Son, in order that he might be the firstborn among many brothers. And those whom he predestined he also called, and those whom he called he also justified, and those whom he justified he also glorified."* The beginning of salvation in these verses is God foreknowing people. He doesn't foreknow something about them, but knows *them* as His elect people. These ones He then called, justified, and glorified. Therefore election is not based on knowing something *about* someone (i.e. that they believe) but knowing them *as people*. Election is unconditional.

- Romans 9:11–13: *"...though they were not yet born and had done nothing either good or bad—in order that God's purpose of election might continue, not because of works but because of him who calls— she was told, 'The older will serve the younger.' As it is written, 'Jacob I loved, but Esau I hated. '''* Here Paul reminds His readers that God's elective purpose is not based on action, but on God who chooses without taking action into account. Before birth and without taking into account good or bad, God elects. Therefore election is once again unconditional. If God were to elect on the merits of the individual, then Jacob would certainly not be the one to elect! The very fact that God chose Jacob who was a deceiver and a cheat shows that God does not take any merit into account and elects without condition.

- 2 Thessalonians 2:13: "*But we ought always to give thanks to God for you, brothers beloved by the Lord, because God chose you as the firstfruits to be saved, through sanctification by the Spirit and belief in the truth.*" God chose us to be saved, plain and simple. In light of the above verses, this verse in Calvinist thought shows that salvation has its roots in the choice of God. He chose us to be saved; we did not choose Him for our salvation.

Limited Atonement (or Particular Redemption)[16]

God's elect people still have a problem: they are still sinners in need of saving from their sin! Logically the next point of Calvinism naturally comes after Unconditional Election.[17] Because we are totally depraved and would never seek God, He must step in for anyone ever to be redeemed. He has done so and elected some to be saved, and those people now need to be redeemed from their sin. If He has decided who He will save, then it only stands to reason that the people that Jesus came to die for are the very same people that God already decided previously to give eternal life to.

Calvinism believes that the purpose and plan of God in Jesus' death and the work Jesus did on the cross (called "atonement"[18]) was to redeem God's chosen people. All are totally depraved and worthy of condemnation, but out of that group God chose to save some by His good pleasure. Therefore, the intent of Christ's death was to pay for the sins of those whom God had already chosen to

---

[16] Ibid., 594–603; Steele, Thomas, and Quinn, *The Five Points of Calvinism*, 39–51; Horton, *For Calvinism*, 80–98.
[17] The fact that it makes the flower acrostic work nicely is a helpful bonus!
[18] Atonement can be defined, according to Grenz, Guretzki, and Nordling, *Pocket Dictionary of Theological Terms*, 17, as "God's act of dealing with the primary human problem, sin. Both OT and NT affirm that sin has broken the relationship between God and humankind. According to Christian theology, God accomplished the way of restoration through Christ's death."

save. (Ephesians 5:25)[19] The atonement, then, is *limited* in its intent. It is intended not to offer salvation to all people without exception, but to actually secure it for those God has already decided are His.

This is not to say that Christ's death did not have sufficient *value* to redeem all of humanity; it was of infinite worth and so was valuable enough to save all people with an infinite amount to spare. It is to say that the *intent* and the *extent* of the atonement are identical. (John 17:9) In other words, because God's purpose was to redeem those who are chosen by God, the target of Christ's death is those elect people and therefore the extent of the atonement is the elect. (Acts 20:28)

To Calvinists, if God paid for the sins of unbelievers it would be unjust to send them to hell because they would be judged for something that Christ was already judged for.[20] Even more, if Jesus died for everyone's sins then the work of Christ would be wasted on many people who never trust Him, which is dishonoring to Christ. God's glory and greatness would be diminished if the work of Christ was wasted, and we must not forget that the greatness and majesty of God is the center of Calvinism's system.

---

[19] In more academic terms, the atonement is logically subsequent to election.
[20] Grudem, *Systematic Theology*, 595.

Limited Atonement speaks not of the worth of Christ's sacrifice but rather of its purpose. Jesus' death within Calvinism doesn't make salvation possible; instead, it actively and completely purchases the salvation of the elect. (2 Corinthians 5:21) It makes the salvation of the elect complete and causes their salvation without being dependent upon some response in people for its effectiveness.[21] God will use faith in Christ as an instrument in their life, but Christ's death surely and completely bought their salvation.

The verses in the paragraphs above are some that Calvinists point to for evidence of limited atonement, but the following are perhaps the most foundational to this idea:

- John 10:11: "*I am the good shepherd. The good shepherd lays down his life for the sheep.*" Here Jesus says that He lays His life down for a particular group, namely the sheep. The image of Jesus as shepherd and His elect as sheep is a tender one. He limits the intent of the sacrifice He will soon give to the ones that He knows beforehand have been given to Him by the Father. The saints that God elected, Christ laid down His life for. He did not lay down His life for any other but the sheep.

---

[21] The means that God uses to bring about the sure salvation of the elect are described in the last two points of Calvinism.

- Romans 8:32: *"He who did not spare his own Son but gave him up for us all, how will he not also with him graciously give us all things?"* This section of Romans deals with the blessings given to those whom God has elected. It comes right after verses 29-30, which in Calvinist thought shows unconditional election. Paul continues his thought by saying that God gave the Son not for all people without distinction, but for believers. The intent in Christ's death was not to save every person without exception, but to save the elect. The intent of Christ's death is limited to the elect.

- Romans 5:8: *"...but God shows his love for us in that while we were still sinners, Christ died for us."* Again, in Romans Paul's focus is on the death of Christ for us, the elect. Christ died for us, not for every person whether they accept Christ or not. Therefore the atonement was only intended to pay for the sins of those whom God elected.

- Romans 5:10: *"For if while we were enemies we were reconciled to God by the death of his Son, much more, now that we are reconciled, shall we be saved by his life."* Within the same context as the previous point, Paul continues with the reconciliation offered by the cross. The consistent approach that Paul uses here is to limit the intent of the atonement to those who actually experience the blessings of eternal life. We were reconciled by the death of His son. Therefore the death of Christ did not make redemption[22] *possible*, but made it a sure fact.

- Galatians 3:13: "*Christ redeemed us from the curse of the law by becoming a curse for us...*" Christ did not redeem everyone, but His death assured the redemption of believers. He became a curse specifically and only for us, the elect. He took our sin upon Himself to pay for our sins, but this does not include those who never experience the benefits of redemption. This is no mere potential; Christ actually redeemed the elect rather than just making redemption from sin possible for anyone.

If someone says that they are a "four point Calvinist," this is the point that they almost certainly don't hold to.[23] More staunch Calvinists argue back that there is no such thing as a four-point Calvinist, because the system holds together as a whole or it falls as a whole. The idea of the intent of the atonement being for those God unconditionally elected is a logical necessity within classic

---

[22] Redemption, according to Grenz, Guretzki, and Nordling, *Pocket Dictionary of Theological Terms*, 100, is "The process by which sinful humans are 'bought back' from the bondage of sin into relationship with God through grace by the 'payment' of Jesus' death."

[23] Whether they hold to the Arminian idea of Universal Atonement or the Molinist idea of Singular Redemption depends on the individual. "Four point" Calvinism is called Amyraldism after Moses Amyraut, who popularized it. For more, see J. Matthew Pinson, ed., *Four Views on Eternal Security* (Grand Rapids, MI: Zondervan, 2002), 113.

Calvinism and is therefore very important to the system, but is certainly the most controversial point in the system.

Irresistible Grace[24]

The next link in the chain of Calvinism is termed *irresistible grace*, though that wording is open to misunderstanding. This term can sound like God puts people under the Imperius curse or uses a Jedi mind trick to force people to come to faith in Christ, but that is not really what this point argues for.[25] Look at this point of Calvinism more like God making salvation so bright and shiny for the elect that it's too good to pass up. It's more like offering a kid a bowl of ice cream than putting a spell on them to like math or something; there's no way they can resist!

This point gets caricatured a lot by opponents. Usually this idea gets tossed about by those who disagree with it as if it amounts to coercion or forcibly bringing people to faith in Christ against their will. However, by this term Calvinists do not mean that God forces anyone to become a Christian, "kicking and screaming." What it does mean is that because God has elected a person and Christ has paid for their sins and redeemed them, He also *will*

---

[24] Grudem, *Systematic Theology*, 699–704; Steele, Thomas, and Quinn, *The Five Points of Calvinism*, 52–63; Horton, *For Calvinism*, 99–109.

[25] Yes, that was both a Harry Potter reference AND a Star Wars reference in a single sentence. You're welcome.

regenerate[26] them. (Romans 8:29-30) Those whom God has "born again" will certainly and absolutely come to faith in Christ; it is not possible that one of the elect will fail to come to trust Christ. They will come willingly, but without question they *will* come. In that sense, God's grace toward the elect is irresistible.

This drawing of the elect to faith in Christ is known as the *effectual call*, in that when the Spirit calls a person to salvation He is always effective in bringing them to trust Christ. While God is glorified by all people hearing the gospel and all being given the call to trust Christ for their eternal life (the general call), only the elect will hear that call in a way that moves them to accept Christ (the effectual call). If God elects someone, He pays for their sins and then at the point in their life when He determines it is appropriate He gives them the gift of faith in Christ. So salvation in Calvinism is all of God, because even faith is a gift from Him.

For this reason, within Calvinism faith is the result of regeneration; God regenerates a person, and therefore they come to faith in Christ. (John 3:5) To Calvinists, if it were the other way around it would amount to faith being a work that we do to earn salvation, and this is never the case! (Ephesians 2:8-9) This is tied closely with God's greatness. Since He is in control of all that comes to

---

[26] Regeneration is, "A biblical motif of salvation that emphasizes the rebirth or re-creation of fallen human beings by the indwelling Holy Spirit."Grenz, Guretzki, and Nordling, *Pocket Dictionary of Theological Terms*, 101.

pass and has decided to elect a person, He uses the means of Christ's death and then grants them the new birth to surely and absolutely bring them to faith in Christ.

In this sense the grace of God in bringing someone to faith in Christ is irresistible. Again it's better to see that irresistibility as being so enticing that it's impossible to resist rather than being coercive.[27] God's irresistible grace given to His children is the basis for our eternal life as clearly stated in the following Scriptures:

- John 1:12-13: *"But to all who did receive him, who believed in his name, he gave the right to become children of God, who were born, not of blood nor of the will of the flesh nor of the will of man, but of God."* John 1:12 tells us that all who trust Christ are children of God and are bound for heaven. Verse 13 clarifies that those who trust Christ are not those who are born from their parents as Christians (no one is), nor are they those who chose Christ of their own will. Rather, those who believe in Christ are born of

---

[27] Some Calvinists even like to use the idea of *compatibilist free will* to describe the way God brings someone to salvation. This means that we have some limited free will, within the confines of our nature. Since we are all totally depraved, our nature before Christ is evil and therefore we would never choose God. However, when God regenerates someone they are given a new nature (2 Corinthians 5:17) and therefore they choose according to this new nature and trust Christ for eternal life.

the will of God. He is the one who elects and therefore draws people to Christ. It is according to His will, not the will of people.

- John 3:3–8: "*Jesus answered him, 'Truly, truly, I say to you, unless one is born again he cannot see the kingdom of God.' Nicodemus said to him, 'How can a man be born when he is old? Can he enter a second time into his mother's womb and be born?' Jesus answered, 'Truly, truly, I say to you, unless one is born of water and the Spirit, he cannot enter the kingdom of God. That which is born of the flesh is flesh, and that which is born of the Spirit is spirit. Do not marvel that I said to you, "You must be born again." The wind blows where it wishes, and you hear its sound, but you do not know where it comes from or where it goes. So it is with everyone who is born of the Spirit.'"* The new birth is not something that comes in a way that we can control or cause, but in a way that is according to God's design and His unique way. In Jesus' words here, God the Holy Spirit goes wherever He wishes and regenerates ("births again") whoever it is His will to bring to faith. Therefore the grace of God is guaranteed to bring someone to Christ.
- John 6:37: "*All that the Father gives me will come to me, and whoever comes to me I will never cast out.*" There is no

doubt in this verse that all who are chosen by God *will* come to faith in Christ. Jesus does not say that they "might" come to Him or that they "can" come to Him, but that they "will" infallibly come to Him. The grace of God in salvation is sure to accomplish its means and is, therefore, irresistible. People who are elect come to Christ not under coercion, but they most certainly will come. There is no doubt of the effectiveness of the call.

- John 6:44: "*No one can come to me unless the Father who sent me draws him. And I will raise him up on the last day.*" (John 6:44, ESV) In the same context as the previous verse, Jesus says that no one would come to God unless the Father makes it happen. Since Jesus says He *will* raise them up on the last day, it means that everyone the Father draws will indeed come to faith in Christ. This makes the electing and regenerating grace of God irresistible.

Perseverance (or Preservation) of the Saints[28]

The final point of Calvinism flows from the first four. If God has regenerated someone and given them the gift of faith, then it only stands to reason that the gift of faith that God gives would be lasting. He doesn't give defective gifts to His children, and the gift

---

[28] Grudem, *Systematic Theology*, 788–809; Steele, Thomas, and Quinn, *The Five Points of Calvinism*, 64–77; Horton, *For Calvinism*, 115–121.

of faith in Christ is the most important gift of all! God will absolutely preserve His children in faith and they will continue by faith in a life of holy conduct that continues and increases. (Hebrews 6:9)

The logic of the Calvinist system of salvation finds its end here. Those whom God has regenerated and given the gift of faith have been redeemed by Christ because they are elect, and because of these truths the gift that they have been given will never go away. It's like God wrote their faith using a permanent marker; once it's written, there's no going back. They will continue in the faith throughout life, persevering in a life of holiness that continues till their last breath. Holiness is the requirement of all of God's children (1 Peter 1:15-16), and God guarantees that the faith that declares them righteous before God is the same faith that makes them more like Him and keeps them firm in His love until death.

This is not to say that Christians will be sinless, or that they cannot sin terribly or even in some sense keep on sinning for some time. Experience shows that Christians can sin seriously and even repetitively. Biblical examples like the Apostle Peter denying Christ and even carrying bigotry with him (Acts 10:1-33; Galatians 2:11-14) show us that Christians are not perfect and still sin. However, the doctrine of the Perseverance of the Saints does mean that all true Christians will desire a life of holiness and growth in

Christ-likeness. It means that if someone walks away from the faith entirely or lives a life of persistent and willful sin without remorse or repentance, then they have not been born again and therefore were never truly converted to begin with. (1 Corinthians 6:9-11)

Not everyone who claims to be a Christian really is, and the Perseverance of the Saints shows in the end who is really saved and who is not. Non-Christians can show many signs of conversion such as doing good works and even seeking in some sense to please God. (Matthew 7:21-23) However, this will not be a lifelong or God-pleasing effort and is self-righteousness. In contrast, true faith always shows itself as a faith that perseveres to the end of life, and no believer can live in persistent, unrepentant sin. (1 John 3:6-9) God ensures that believers will live holy lives, and the mark of regeneration is personal holiness. (James 2:14-26)

There are several Scriptures that point to the need for truly regenerate people to live their lives in a God-honoring way. The following verses are given special weight in the discussion because of their clarity:

- John 8:31–32: *"So Jesus said to the Jews who had believed him, "If you abide in my word, you are truly my disciples, and you will know the truth, and the truth will set you free."*

Jesus' disciples abide in His word. Only His disciples will abide in His word, and His disciples *will* abide in His word. The logical opposite of this verse is that those who do *not* abide in the word of Christ (i.e. are disobedient to Christ) are not His disciples and are therefore unsaved. Since God saves the elect without losing any, someone who ends up not abiding in the word of Christ was not elect and never truly believed in Christ.

- Colossians 1:21–23: "*And you, who once were alienated and hostile in mind, doing evil deeds, he has now reconciled in his body of flesh by his death, in order to present you holy and blameless and above reproach before him, if indeed you continue in the faith, stable and steadfast, not shifting from the hope of the gospel that you heard, which has been proclaimed in all creation under heaven, and of which I, Paul, became a minister.*" The condition of being presented before Christ in Colossians 1 is that we continue in the faith. If we fall away from the faith, we will not be presented before Christ as His children because we have not persevered. That lack of perseverance in Christ shows that we were never saved to begin with. Those who are reconciled to God through Christ continue in the faith until the end of life.

- Hebrews 3:14: *"For we have come to share in Christ, if indeed we hold our original confidence firm to the end."* If we do not hold our confidence in Christ firm until the end, it is clear that we do not "share" in Christ. That means that we are not among the elect and therefore are unsaved. Those whom God has regenerated will hold their confidence firm in Christ throughout life to the very end. It is the mark of true conversion and without perseverance in the faith we have no assurance or hope of eternal life. If a person doesn't continue in the faith, they were never given the gift of faith from God and whatever they had was not a biblical, saving faith.

- 1 Corinthians 15:1–2: *"Now I would remind you, brothers, of the gospel I preached to you, which you received, in which you stand, and by which you are being saved, if you hold fast to the word I preached to you…"* Being saved requires that believers hold fast to the gospel that they received from the Apostles. Clearly, because of the doctrines of unconditional election and irresistible grace, true believers are regenerated and given a new nature in order to do this. God is the one who guarantees it! If we let go of the words of the Apostles and leave the faith, then it shows that we are not being saved at the current time and therefore we are not saved.

Strengths and Concerns of Calvinism

Calvinism can be easily remembered by considering their flower:
TULIP. Calvinists believe in the doctrines of Total Depravity,
Unconditional Election, Limited Atonement, Irresistible Grace,
and the Perseverance of the Saints. Their garden grows with God's
sovereign work, and ONLY with God's work, from start to finish.
God uses faith, which is a gift He gives His children, as the means
to bring someone into a right relationship with Him and then keep
that relationship secure throughout life and into eternity. God
plants and cultivates the TULIP without any merit on our part,
highlighting His greatness and control over history and creation.

The five points of TULIP are the bedrock of Calvinism. They
form a tightly-knit system that proceeds from our problem as
people (total depravity) to God's solution to that problem from
start to finish. Like every system of theology, Calvinism has its
strengths and weaknesses.[29] Recognizing the strengths and
weaknesses of each system is critical to deciding which flower we
want to plant in our garden!

---

[29] More to come on this in chapter 4. It would be great if one system or the
other had all the strengths and none of the weaknesses, but this is not reality. If
one system or the other had all the strengths and none of the weaknesses it
would have long ago won the hearts and minds of all Christians! Alas, the
theological "Hunger Games" are still ongoing, and no champion has been
crowned.

Strengths

+   God, the One who is the "unmoved mover"[30], does all the work in TULIP. He gets all the glory because He is responsible for everything that happens from start to finish. There is certainly no room for anyone to boast in Calvinism about their salvation! (Romans 3:27)

+   Because of this, Calvinism is heavy on the sovereignty of God and His perfect control of the world and events in the world. The greatness of God is the center of the system. What God wants to happen, happens! (Isaiah 46:10) Therefore evangelism and outreach are not dependent upon our efforts (even though God chooses to use our work in evangelism to bring people to Christ). God *will* bring the elect to faith, and that should bring us peace. No one will be lost because of our ineptitude.

+   Calvinism has (relative) history. John Calvin was one of the preeminent Protestant Reformers, and his theology and understanding of Scripture took the Reformation to heights that would never have happened without him. Since Calvin, many have followed his lead including historical greats such as Jonathan Edwards and Charles Spurgeon.

---

[30] Aristotle, *Aristotle in 23 Volumes*, trans. Hugh Tredennick, vol. 17, 18 (Cambridge, MA: Harvard University Press, 1933), Book 12. 1072b .

+ In the hearts of many who are Calvinists, the model gives peace because God is in control. If He is in control of all of history and especially if decisions are in God's hands, then everything that happens is the will of God and believers can rest, confident that God is doing what brings Him glory. Being among the elect brings peace and joy.

+ Calvinism has many esteemed modern pastors and scholars who hold its tenets. Pastors like John Piper, John MacArthur, Mark Driscoll, and Francis Chan are high-profile and vocal proponents. Scholars who are Calvinists include Piper, RC Sproul, and Al Mohler among many.

Concerns

− The problem of God's justice and mercy. If God is the one who does it all, why not elect everyone? Why create those who reject Him? Calvinists answer that we are not to question God's elective purposes (Romans 9:20), but this for many is an unsatisfactory answer. Saying that the purpose of those who aren't elect is for God's greater glory can make God sound like an egomaniac and terribly malicious.

- The problem of suffering.[31] If determinism is true and God sovereignly causes all decisions and all actions, then how can God be good and allow such innocent suffering? Even if we are allowed a "soft determinism," where God allows us the freedom to choose according to our desires (which are evil when we are unregenerate), the onus is still on God to be the author of evil and suffering. This is a thorny concern if there is no free will among humans, and one that is difficult for many non-Calvinists to accept.

- The problem of assurance. If someone can *think* they are saved but might fall away later and prove that they never really *were* saved, then any assurance of salvation is elusive at best and impossible at worst. This seems to have plagued some of the great reformers, even men as great as Martin Luther.

- The purpose and intent of the atonement. Though logically it is required within Calvinism, the weight of Scripture seems to say that the intent of the atonement is wider than Calvinism would argue.[32]

---

[31] Perhaps one of the best resources for someone interested in studying the problem of evil from a theological and philosophical perspective is Mark Larrimore, *The Problem of Evil: A Reader*, 1st ed. (Hoboken, NJ: Wiley-Blackwell, 2000). It's fairly hefty but offers an excellent introduction to evil from a biblical view.

[32] We shall see this in the discussion on Arminianism.

– Free will and honest relationship. Many statements in Scripture seem to point to human beings having significant moral decision-making power, including over eternal life. A total denial of that leaves many passages of Scripture needing to be qualified and categorized.

If you'd like to read more about Calvinism, there are several good books that are helpful for understanding the system from their perspective:

John Calvin, *Institutes of the Christian Religion*, Revised. (Peabody, MA; Hendrickson Publishers, Inc., 2007). This is not a simple book nor easy for a modern reader to understand unless they have a pretty significant background in theology, but if you want classic Calvinism then this is the place to go.

Mark Driscoll and Gerry Breshears, *Doctrine: What Christians Should Believe* (Wheaton, IL: Crossway, 2011). This book is written for regular people to read, so it's a helpful tool for understanding Calvinism. It's not just about salvation but a wider understanding of basic doctrinal principles in line with Calvinism.

Wayne Grudem, *Systematic Theology: An Introduction to Biblical Doctrine* (Grand Rapids, MI; Zondervan, 1994).

This book is the standard systematic theology used in Calvinist Bible colleges and seminaries. It's hefty but easy to read.

Michael S. Horton, *For Calvinism* (Grand Rapids, MI; Zondervan, 2011). This is one of the better books on Calvinism around. It is easy to read, very helpful, and kind in its approach.

Robert A. Peterson and Michael D. Williams, *Why I Am Not an Arminian* (Downers Grove, IL; IVP Books, 2004).

R. C. Sproul, *What is Reformed Theology?: Understanding the Basics* (Grand Rapids, MI; Baker Books, 2005).

David N. Steele, Curtis C. Thomas, and S. Lance Quinn, *The Five Points of Calvinism: Defined, Defended, and Documented*, 2nd ed. (Phillipsburg, NJ; P & R Publishing, 2004).

There are certainly some significant reasons that many want TULIPs in their garden! At the same time, the concerns with Calvinism are significant enough that many others understand the way Scripture presents salvation in a different light. The first and most major alternative system to Calvinism was first proposed by a student of John Calvin's successor (and son-in-law!), and it gets our attention next.

Questions for Individual Thought and Group Discussion:

1. Which letter of TULIP do you think has the best evidence? Why is it strong?

2. Which letter of TULIP do you think has the most challenges? What are its weaknesses?

3. What do you think of Calvinism's central idea of God's greatness? Do you think that there is enough evidence in Scripture to make this the central idea of God in salvation? Why or why not?

4. Before starting this study, would you have considered yourself a Calvinist? Would you now? Why or why not?

5. Limited Atonement is the most controversial point of Calvinism. Would you say that it undermines the goodness of God to only want to save the elect, or does it make His love more personal and special for those who are saved?

6. If you're not a Calvinist, which point can you respect the most? If you are, which point do you think is most difficult for non-Calvinists to appreciate?

Chapter 3: Arminianism-Growing LILACs

Our next flower is pretty in its own right, but has some significant distinctions from the TULIP we saw in Calvinism. We must really understand what the differences are (and understand what they are not) to compare and contrast them. Unfortunately, many people who aren't Arminian don't understand classic Arminianism well, and you can't evaluate what you don't understand. Several acrostics are popular for understanding Arminian theology, but the best and easiest to understand is LILAC.[1] This pretty flower grows in the gardens of many Christians around the world today.

In Arminianism, God is in charge of everything but we plant the flowers with Him.[2] We have significant responsibility in the garden of Arminianism for planting LILACs! God does this not because we're so important but because His goodness is the center of Arminian theology. God is good, so He lets us help plant the

---

[1] Many Calvinists like to use the acrostic DAISY to describe Arminianism, but unfortunately that acrostic is used many times to attack the position more than understand it. The caricature gets used because, as a joke, some say that the Arminian picks petals off the daisy and thinks of God, "He loves me…He loves me not" as a jab at their understanding of the security of the believer. That's not nice, so we will instead focus on a different acrostic that gives the same information without the potential for misunderstandings.

[2] As opposed to Calvinism's monergism (see above), Arminianism sees salvation as synergism. This term comes from the Greek prefix *syn-* ("with") and the noun *ergos* ("work") and means that we cooperate with God to accomplish salvation. God does the work, we cooperate, and salvation is achieved.

flowers. We plant LILACs because God in His goodness allows us to be part of the planting process.

We must also make sure that we differentiate between Arminians and Armenians. "Armenian" with an e is a designation for people from Armenia or a member of the church started by St. Gregory in the 4th Century. "Arminian" with an i is a designation for a system of understanding salvation. Not all Armenians are Arminian, and many (most?) Arminians are not Armenian![3] The trick to remember is that the Arminian theology is spelled with an i, as in "**I** choose God," while Armenian people are spelled with an e, as in "they are an **e**thnic group." We are not interested in comparing ethnic groups, but in theologies, so we will keep our focus on Arminianism.

Arminianism as a system follows the teaching of Jacob Arminius (1560-1609). Arminius studied for a time under Theodore Beza, a disciple of John Calvin and his successor in Geneva. Arminius reacted to the teaching of Calvinism, forming an alternative system of understanding salvation focused on the offer of salvation to all people rather than the decree of God to save some and not others. Arminianism found a branching point in the teaching of John

---

[3] Making this common spelling error makes you look like a doofus in theological discussions too.

Wesley, and Wesleyan Arminianism is a distinct branch of Arminianism with its own distinctives and focus.

There are several denominations and groups that would fall under the title of "Arminian" today. All Pentecostal denominations trace their roots to Wesleyan Arminianism. The largest Pentecostal (and therefore Arminian) denomination in America is the Assemblies of God. Restorationists such as the Church of Christ, Independent Christian Churches and Disciples of Christ are at their core Arminian. Methodism and its offshoots in the Holiness movement (such as the Church of the Nazarene), and many Baptist denominations (such as the American Baptist Association and the Free Will Baptists) are also Arminian.[4] In fact, many denominations that identify as "not Calvinist" (for lack of a better term) in one way or another are more or less Arminian in their understanding.

The center of Arminian theology is not so much the free will of people as it is the goodness of God. While many who are not Arminian say that free will is the center of Arminian thought, this is really not the case. Free will is the consequence in Arminian thought of the goodness of God. Because the central idea within Arminianism is that God is good and loving, He provides people

---

[4] There are many different kinds of Baptists, and some are more Calvinist and others like those mentioned here are more Arminian.

with the ability to respond to His revelation despite their fallen state. God's goodness is so big that, even though we are fallen and depraved, He has left enough of His image within us that we can still trust Christ for eternal life. Free will is a consequence of God's goodness toward us.

Just as with Calvinism, the diverse groups that make up Arminian theology lead to diverse theological positions and therefore it can be difficult to find a single picture of Arminian theology.[5] Just like with Calvinism, though, Arminians have written enough to be able to say what the broad understanding of salvation from their perspective looks like. The Remonstrance, a document by Arminians to point out errors they believed were present in Calvinism, may prove helpful to understanding the points of Arminianism as a whole[6]:

---

[5] Olson, *Arminian Theology*, 12 states that as late as 2006 that there was no book that he was aware of in English and in print solely dedicated to describing classic Arminianism as a system of theology. There are certainly books out there like I. Howard Marshall, *New Testament Theology: Many Witnesses, One Gospel* (Downers Grove, IL: IVP Academic, 2004). This, like many others, is less a systematic look than it is a look through each book of the New Testament to see what it says about various theological issues. If you're interested in the historical development of Arminianism and other branches of the western church, a great resource is Susan L. Peterson, Hannah, John D., and Holden, Joseph, *Timeline Charts of the Western Church* (Grand Rapids, MI: Zondervan, 1999).

[6] A. W. Harrison, *The Beginnings of Arminianism to the Synod of Dort,*, First ed. (University of London Press, 1926), 151.

1. That God, by an eternal and unchangeable decree in Christ before the world was, determined to elect from the fallen and sinning race to everlasting life those who through His grace believe in Jesus Christ and persevere in faith and obedience; and, on the contrary, had resolved to reject the unconverted and unbelievers to everlasting damnation (John iii, 36).

2. That, in consequence of this, Christ the Saviour of the world died for all and every man, so that He obtained, by the death on the cross, reconciliation and pardon for sin for all men; in such manner, however, that none but the faithful actually enjoyed the same (John iii, 16; 1 John ii, 2).

3. That man could not obtain saving faith of himself or by the strength of his own free will, but stood in need of God's grace through Christ to be renewed in thought and will (John xv, 5).

4. That this grace was the cause of the beginning, progress and completion of man's salvation; insomuch that none could believe nor persevere in faith without this co-operating grace, and consequently that all good works must be ascribed to the grace of God in Christ. As to the manner of the operation of that grace, however, it is not irresistible (Acts vii, 51).

5. That true believers had sufficient strength through the Divine grace to fight against Satan, sin, the world, their own flesh, and get the victory over them; but whether by negligence they might not apostatize from the true Faith, lose the happiness of a good conscience and forfeit that grace needed to be more fully inquired into according to Holy Writ.

Clearly, there are some distinctives that Arminianism holds in contrast to Calvinism. A more modern treatment and discussion of the pattern of the five points of Calvinism proves helpful from a classically Arminian perspective as well.[7] What is worth noting is that Arminian theology agrees in some sense with the T and the P of the Reformed acrostic TULIP; in the ULI in the middle, though, there is significant difference of understanding.

The Arminian flower is different than the Calvinist flower, but no less pretty and certainly deserves our attention. While Calvinists prefer TULIPs, Arminians prefer to plant LILACs: **L**imited Depravity, **I**ndividual Responsibility, **L**imitless Atonement,

---

[7] The classical position is covered well by Olson, *Arminian Theology*. This discussion will draw on his work as a standard-bearer for the position. Another helpful book is Roger E. Olson, *Against Calvinism* (Grand Rapids, MI: Zondervan, 2011). Finally, an excellent critique of Calvinism that sets out the Arminian (or more appropriately, the "non-Calvinist") position is David L. Allen and Steve W. Lemke, eds., *Whosoever Will: A Biblical-Theological Critique of Five-Point Calvinism* (Nashville, TN: B&H Academic, 2010).

Arrestable Grace, and Conditional Security.[8] Keep the acrostic LILAC in your mind as we consider what each letter in the flower stands for in Arminian theology.

Limited Depravity[9]

First off, to be clear Arminians *do* believe in total depravity in some sense. "Arminianism teaches that all humans are born morally and spiritually depraved, and helpless to do anything good or worthy in God's sight without a special infusion of God's grace to overcome the affects of original sin."[10] This sounds quite Calvinistic! Humans, as a result of the fall, are affected in their entire beings and are unable to avoid sin or the penalty of sin. We are completely sinful and can do nothing but sin without the supernatural work of God in our lives.[11]

So we must first be very clear about this: Arminians accept the *idea* of total depravity. They agree with all of the Calvinist explanation that, left on their own, people would never turn to God. They accept the Scriptures that say that we are dead in our

---

[8] I have not seen a treatment of LILAC that uses the exact words I do for the acrostic, but the way that I am explaining it here should help readers without a strong theological background understand this system in distinction from Calvinism well.

[9] Olson, *Arminian Theology*, 33; Olson, *Against Calvinism*, 70–101; Allen and Lemke, *Whosoever Will*, 29–44.

[10] Ibid.

[11] Ibid, 34.

trespasses and sins (Ephesians 2:1) and unwilling to seek after God. (Romans 3:11) However, it is equally clear to Arminians that the story of our depravity and the effects of depravity don't end there.

Where Arminianism departs from Calvinism on depravity is in the idea known as *prevenient grace*. Unlike the Calvinist idea of *common grace* (which Arminians believe in as well), prevenient grace is the grace of God that He has poured out on humanity, through the work of Christ. Because of Jesus' death on the cross and the work of the Holy Spirit in the world, people are prompted by God in grace to desire to please God and given understanding concerning God's will. In some sense it overcomes the effects of the Fall, providing the means to respond to the Gospel. As Miracle Max said in the movie "The Princess Bride," we're only *mostly* dead.

God's prevenient grace therefore creates free will. Because of God's universal work in the world to bring people to Himself, we have been given an irresistible grace[12] by Him to have the choice to accept or reject Christ. (Luke 13:34) God in His goodness gives this gift to all people. It is given to all people to make the Gospel

---

[12] See, that's a term Calvinists like to use a lot! Arminians like to talk about "irresistible grace" too, but give it a definition or use that is different. It's all very postmodern, really, but don't tell them that.

understandable and acceptable, though it is still their responsibility to respond.

> For Wesley (and consequently for many Arminians)
> prevenient grace is the Holy Spirit's work in the
> hearts of all people, which gives them the freedom
> to say yes to the gospel; thus prevenient grace can
> be accepted or rejected, but justification cannot be
> achieved without it.[13]

In other words, though we are totally depraved on our own, God doesn't leave us alone. He stepped into the world in the Person of Jesus to pay for the sins of all people, and because of this grace we all have the ability to respond to God. (John 3:16) So our depravity, while in some sense total (or maybe complete is a better word), has been overridden by God to restore us to some form of free will. The Holy Spirit works within each person to convict them, to woo them, and to let them hear the Gospel clearly. (John 16:8) It is this convicting and convincing work of the Spirit that gives us the free will to accept Christ, though we can still reject Him if we want to.

There are many Scriptures that seem to point to a limit to human depravity. They say that God is the one who must take the

---

[13] Grenz, Guretzki, and Nordling, *Pocket Dictionary of Theological Terms*, 95.

initiative, but that humans have a truly meaningful role to play. Some of the more significant verses are:

- Ezekiel 34:11, 16: *"For thus says the Lord GOD: Behold, I, I myself will search for my sheep and will seek them out…I will seek the lost, and I will bring back the strayed, and I will bind up the injured, and I will strengthen the weak…"* To Arminians, this verse speaks of the Lord's searching for people, especially the "lost" and the "strayed." Those who are outside the family of God are those who God is looking for, which shows His care for all.

- Luke 19:10: *"For the Son of Man came to seek and to save the lost."* It is not the elect that Christ came to find, but the lost. This has some element of condition to it; in other words, the lost must respond to the seeking of Jesus.

- John 6:44: *"No one can come to me unless the Father who sent me draws him."* To an Arminian, Jesus in John 6 is saying that no one has the ability to come to the Father unless the Father draws them. This He has done with prevenient grace! It would be impossible for someone to come to God on their own, but God universally draws people to Christ through the wooing of the Spirit and the proclamation of the Word. In fact, the word translated "draws" is most likely, in this context, speaking of the

Father "wooing" rather than forcing someone to come to Christ or drawing them without fail or decision on their part.[14]

- John 12:32: *"And I, when I am lifted up from the earth, will draw all people to myself."* This is a strong statement that says that Christ's crucifixion draws not just the elect, but "all people" to Jesus. This does not, of course, mean that all people will actually come to faith in Christ, but that Jesus' death is the means that the Father uses to pour out grace on all of humanity and give them the ability to accept Christ.

- In addition to these verses, Arminians argue that the many commands to believe in Christ in the Scriptures, given to unbelievers, shows that God expects unbelievers to trust Christ. They must therefore have the ability to trust Christ, which is evidence that God has given them that ability. Their explanation of that ability is not the *irresistible grace* of Calvinism which invariably draws the elect, but *prevenient grace* given to all to make salvation possible.

---

[14] David R. Anderson, *Free Grace Soteriology* (n.p.: Xulon Press, 2010), 237–239. Anderson is not Arminian in a classical sense, but his explanation of the argument of this particular verse is quite good in this verse from the standpoint of someone who believes that people have free will.

Individual Responsibility[15]

Arminians react pretty strongly to the Calvinist idea of unconditional election because to them it calls the character of God into question. Within Arminian theology, the goodness of God is always front and center, and to them the idea that God chooses some just because He wants to and sends the rest to hell is unthinkable. It makes God a moral monster! Within Arminian theology, anyone who is damned to hell is only damned to hell because of their own rejection of Christ.

That said, Arminians do uphold the principle of election and predestination because they are biblical.[16] They don't reject the biblical concepts, though they do reject the Calvinist understanding of how those biblical concepts work. Here is where our responsibility and God's being in charge ("sovereignty") meet, in election that is all of God because of choices that are all of people's own doing.

Within classical Arminianism, because Jesus' death on the cross provided an unlimited atonement the gospel message is open to all.[17] Therefore, God's election of people is based not on His

---

[15] Olson, *Arminian Theology*, 35; Olson, *Against Calvinism*, 102–135; Allen and Lemke, *Whosoever Will*, 45–60.

[16] Olson, *Arminian Theology*, 19.

[17] It is worth noting that, in many ways, while the Calvinist acrostic TULIP proceeds logically from first to last, in many ways Arminianism proceeds

sovereign, uncaused decision but upon His perfect and complete knowledge of all that will come to pass.[18] God looks down the corridors of time, before time ever begins, and chooses to elect all those who He foreknows will place faith in Christ for eternal life. (Romans 8:28-30) The offer of salvation is available to all people without distinction, and God elects those whom He foreknows will respond to the gospel offer.

Because God has not completely wiped out the ability to choose in depraved people so that they cannot respond to Christ, Arminians believe in the concept of free will. This free will is called *libertarian* free will, in that the person has liberty to choose contrary to what they actually did.[19] For example, if a person chooses to eat a roast beef sandwich for lunch they had the ability to choose to have egg salad or skip lunch altogether. The choice was theirs. Likewise, when discussing salvation people are given the ability by God (because of prevenient grace) to accept or reject the Gospel; they have the free will to decide one way or another.

---

logically in the opposite direction. That said, it's easier for our study to work through the doctrines in the same order in both Calvinism and Arminianism to be able to compare them more easily.

[18] The theological term for this is "omniscience," or God's knowledge of all things.

[19] Don't confuse this with politics. Arminians do not necessarily line up with the Libertarian Party, which is an entirely separate concept. Of course, Arminians believe that they have the God-given ability to decide for themselves which political party to align with!

Unlike the Calvinist understanding of God causing salvation, Arminians prefer the idea of *influence* by God and *response* by people.[20] God opens our hearts to be able to believe, but it is still our responsibility to believe. (Acts 16:14) God counts the act of an individual to believe as their choice, and therefore that choice is a genuine one. (Romans 4:3-5) Jesus says that His desire for people will not override their choice of whether to listen to Him or not. (Matthew 23:27)

It is God who always takes the first step, but the individual is always responsible for their choice and is therefore free to make that choice. (Acts 16:31) For God to make people responsible for and accountable for believing in Christ while at the same time knowing they don't have the ability to trust Him[21], makes God into a moral villain and the very opposite of goodness to an Arminian. Since the goodness of God is the center of Arminian salvation, this is unthinkable to an Arminian!

This individual responsibility, to Arminians, is a result of God's goodness and is especially clear in these verses:

- Matthew 11:28: *"Come to me, all who labor and are heavy laden, and I will give you rest."* Note that it is the

---

[20] F. Leroy Forlines, *Classical Arminianism*, ed. J. Matthew Pinson (Nashville, TN; Randall House Publications, 2011), 47.

[21] Remember, within Calvinism's understanding of total depravity, we would never choose God on our own, so He gives the ones He chooses the gift of faith.

responsibility of the person who is heavy laden and is laboring to come to Jesus so they can receive rest from Him. He invites all people to come to Him, and those who do, do so because they choose to. Here we see an open invitation dependent upon the choice of the individual.

- Matthew 23:37: "*"O Jerusalem, Jerusalem, the city that kills the prophets and stones those who are sent to it! How often would I have gathered your children together as a hen gathers her brood under her wings, and you were not willing!"* Jesus states His desire as God made flesh, and here He explicitly says that His desire is not accomplished because the people were not willing. They were the ones responsible for their upcoming judgment, not Jesus. They had individual responsibility before God to use their free will to honor God, and they chose not to. They had responsibility and the freedom to go with it.

- John 3:16: "*For God so loved the world, that he gave his only Son, that whoever believes in him should not perish but have eternal life.*" God loved the world in this verse. The world in John's gospel refers to everything that is hostile to God and places itself against Him, and He loves them! He loves them so much that He sent Christ. That sending was with a purpose, namely that whoever believes in Christ would have eternal life. The offer is open to all people, and those who respond to the offer of eternal life that Christ gives receive the gift of eternal life.

- Romans 8:29: *"For those whom he foreknew he also predestined to be conformed to the image of his Son, in order that he might be the firstborn among many brothers."* God certainly foreknows those who will trust Christ. It is this foreknowledge of the free decisions of people that God uses in election to decide who will spend eternity with Him. He sees their decision and elects all who will put faith alone in Christ alone.

- 1 Timothy 2:3–4: *"This is good, and it is pleasing in the sight of God our Savior, who desires all people to be saved and to come to the knowledge of the truth."* This verse only makes sense if it is an honest expression of God's intent. If God's desire is for all to be saved, then He has given them enough information (the Gospel) as well as the ability to do what He requires (trust Christ) or this verse makes no sense. To an Arminian this verse makes no sense from a Calvinistic perspective; if God desires all people to be saved, and He chooses who will be saved unconditionally, then either all are saved or this verse is wrong. Neither of those are good alternatives! God truly desires all to be saved, and so has given them the ability to believe so that they can be saved.

- 2 Peter 3:9: "*The Lord is not slow to fulfill his promise as some count slowness, but is patient toward you, not wishing that any should perish, but that all should reach repentance.*" God does not desire the destruction of any person. That is truly their choice, but in His goodness God desires all to be saved. Again, this view makes no sense for Arminians if a Calvinist approach is adopted, because then God is either lying to us (by saying that He wishes for all to reach repentance when He has not chosen that), or God is not able to make that happen and is therefore not really great and in charge. It makes better sense to Arminians to say that it is not His ultimate choice but their honest rejection of Him that causes unbelievers to be sent to hell. In so doing they go against the wishes of God.

Limitless Atonement[22]

Both Calvinism and Arminianism agree that the death of Christ has enough value in God's eyes to purchase the salvation of all people. Jesus, God who took on flesh, died for our sins. Because of His perfect nature, perfect obedience to God, and perfect death on the

---

[22] Olson, *Arminian Theology*, 64–69; Olson, *Against Calvinism*, 136–154; Allen and Lemke, *Whosoever Will*, 61–108. Usually the term that theologians like for this is "Unlimited Atonement" (to distinguish from Calvinism's "Limited Atonement") but LIUAC is not a pretty flower!

cross, Jesus' death has infinite worth in the eyes of God. (Matthew 27:54)

The difference in understanding on the death of Christ is what God intended it to provide. Within Calvinism, the intent of the death of Jesus was to save the elect. That was all it was intended to do, so the *intent* of the atonement therefore matches its *extent*. Arminianism, though, believes that the intent of God was to provide the opportunity for salvation to all people, and because of that the benefits of the death of Jesus are extended to all people. Thus Christ died to pay for the sins of both those who accept Christ and those who reject Him.

This is an important difference. In Arminianism, Jesus died for the sins of all people. (Luke 23:34) Because of His goodness, God made a way for all people to come to know His love and forgiveness in Christ. Christ's death covers all people, at least potentially. Whether someone accepts Christ or not, His death is an offering to God on their behalf. Because they have individual responsibility (free will), it would be unjust for God not to provide a way for them to exercise that and be saved. God is completely just, though, so Christ died for their sins to make the choice a significant and valuable one.

This Arminian belief leads some to say that Arminians must believe that everyone goes to heaven, because Jesus died for their sins. This concept, called universalism, is not an accurate understanding of Arminian theology. Instead, they hold that the benefits of the atonement are only *applied* to those who trust Christ. In other words, Christ's death makes the forgiveness of sins possible because it is offered to all as their payment. They must still accept the payment that Christ made for them in order to actually have their sins forgiven.

While Calvinism believes that the atonement is limited in scope, Arminianism believes that the atonement is limited in effectiveness. In other words, it saves only those who accept the death of Christ on their behalf by faith.[23] It is not limited in intent or extent, but in effectiveness based on the response of people to the Gospel. Again, God's goodness means that Christ's death is sufficient to pay for the sins of all people, regardless of their acceptance of Christ. (1 John 2:2) This makes the Gospel truly open to all people.

For an Arminian this is very important, especially in evangelism. To them, if Calvinism's idea of limited atonement is true it means by necessity that the Gospel is really not genuinely offered to all people. Sure, people might be genuine in their presentation of the

---

[23] Ibid, 65.

Gospel when telling someone about Jesus, but that presentation is not really genuine in God's eyes because if they are not elect then Christ didn't die for their sins and they really can't trust Christ and be saved. For the Arminian this is cruel. Instead, they hold that they can stand before every person on earth and honestly present the Gospel message, telling people that Jesus died for their sins and wants them to trust Him for eternal life. (John 3:16)

There are several Scriptures that seem to say that Jesus' death was not intended only for the elect, but was intended for the entire human race. Some of the clearer ones are:

- John 1:29: *"The next day he saw Jesus coming toward him, and said, "Behold, the Lamb of God, who takes away the sin of the world!"* John the Baptist was preaching a baptism of repentance, bringing Israel to a place of readiness for their Messiah. When he saw the Messiah, John's reaction was to look at Jesus and make his listeners understand that the reach of His ministry clearly extended beyond Israel to the whole world.[24] The "world" in John refers to those who are not part of God's people, and so what John, a prophet of

---

[24] As a more advanced discussion, many Calvinists are also "covenant theologians," in whose eyes the church is true spiritual Israel. If that approach is adopted, then John's statement is even more an indication of a limitless atonement because he is clearly talking about Jesus being the one who takes the sins away of more than God's chosen people!

God, told his listeners was that Jesus' sacrifice will pay for the sins of everyone.

- 1 Timothy 2:3–6: *"This is good, and it is pleasing in the sight of God our Savior, who desires all people to be saved and to come to the knowledge of the truth. For there is one God, and there is one mediator between God and men, the man Christ Jesus, who gave himself as a ransom for all, which is the testimony given at the proper time."* Not only does God desire all to be saved, but Jesus gave Himself as a ransom for all. That is an inclusive term. In context of Jesus being the only mediator between God and people, His sacrifice for all is a sacrifice for all people. Therefore the atonement is limitless in its intent.

- 1 Timothy 4:10: *"For to this end we toil and strive, because we have our hope set on the living God, who is the Savior of all people, especially of those who believe."* Here, Paul argues that Jesus is the Savior of all people, whether they trust Christ or not. To be their Savior, He must have died for their sins. Therefore He died for more than those who will experience the benefits of His death, i.e. "those who believe."

- 1 John 2:2: *"He is the propitiation[25] for our sins, and not for ours only but also for the sins of the whole world."* John is writing to believers in this book (1 John 2:12) and he reminds them here that Jesus' death is bigger than they can imagine. Jesus died not just for believers, but for every man, woman, and child who ever lived. The atonement is limitless in extent and intent.

- 2 Peter 2:1: *"But false prophets also arose among the people, just as there will be false teachers among you, who will secretly bring in destructive heresies, even denying the Master who bought them, bringing upon themselves swift destruction."* The atonement is so broad in scope it even extends to those who deny Christ. Here the false prophets mentioned deny Christ, and are therefore unbelievers by definition. Despite that, Peter reminds his readers that Christ bought these false prophets! The intent of the atonement, then, is in God's eyes far broader than just the elect but extends to unbelievers as well.

---

[25] "An offering that turns away the wrath of God directed against sin." Grenz, Guretzki, and Nordling, *Pocket Dictionary of Theological Terms*, 96.

Arrestable Grace[26]

When many of us think about the word "arrestable," our minds go to the world of law enforcement. When someone does something bad enough to get arrested, it's called an "arrestable" offense. When someone is arrested, they are prevented from doing what they were doing and denied freedom to do it. That's a good analogy to the Arminian idea of "arrestable grace." Though God the Holy Spirit works within each person to bring them to faith in Christ, people can still arrest that work and resist His calling.

Because Arminians value the genuinely personal nature of the relationship between God and people, they believe that it is supremely important that the relationship not be forced in any way. Forcing a relationship sounds very emotionally abusive! To make the salvation relationship irresistible, Arminians believe, would violate the very nature of love and make God arbitrary if not monstrous by not bringing all people to saving faith. If there is no place for the free response of people then there is no good reason that all people are not saved. Hence, to Arminians, for God to unconditionally elect and irresistibly draw *without* doing so for everyone is an attack on the goodness and love of God.

---

[26] Olson, *Arminian Theology*, 63–66; Olson, *Against Calvinism*, 155–174; Allen and Lemke, *Whosoever Will*, 109–162.

Remember, Arminians believe in *libertarian free will*.[27] Within this concept, God always allows people the ability to choose other than they did. Since the Holy Spirit is a Person and not an impersonal force, He can be resisted and ignored. (1 Thessalonians 5:19) He can be grieved, and that grief comes when people resist His desires for them. (Ephesians 4:30) Because of God's prevenient grace which is given to all people, they have the grace-enabled and grace-initiated ability not only to accept the gospel but to reject it as well.

This is the way that God worked in the Old Testament as well as in the New. In the Old Testament, God did not force the Israelites to sacrifice the Passover lamb in Exodus 12:1-28. He commanded them to do so, and to paint the blood of the lamb on the doorposts of their homes to avoid the punishment on Egypt. It was up to them to follow through on His command, though. It was their choice in obeying God that led to their deliverance. Likewise, in Matthew 4:18-22 Jesus calls people to follow Him, but He does not force them to. It is their responsibility to respond to the call.

These Scriptures are appealing, but there are more. Several Scriptures point to people being called out for their unwillingness to listen to the call of God upon their lives with disastrous

---

[27] Olson, *Arminian Theology*, 75–76.

consequences, and these especially speak of the ability of people to effectively resist the call of God on them to trust Christ:

- Joshua 24:15: *"And if it is evil in your eyes to serve the Lord, choose this day whom you will serve, whether the gods your fathers served in the region beyond the River, or the gods of the Amorites in whose land you dwell. But as for me and my house, we will serve the Lord.""* Joshua commands the people to serve the Lord, but then says that the choice to do so is in their hands. They will not be forced into serving the Lord; they must choose. The grace that God has lavished upon them is arrestable.

- Luke 7:29–30: *"When all the people heard this, and the tax collectors too, they declared God just, having been baptized with the baptism of John, but the Pharisees and the lawyers rejected the purpose of God for themselves, not having been baptized by him."* The issue here is the purpose of God for the Pharisees and lawyers. Clearly in the context of Luke 7, these guys are bad dudes who hate Jesus. They are against Him and headed to hell. What Luke tells us is that they rejected God's purpose for themselves. They rejected God's purpose! God had a purpose for them, but they arrested that purpose and rejected it. Therefore their damnation is their own fault.

- Luke 13:34: *"O Jerusalem, Jerusalem, the city that kills the prophets and stones those who are sent to it! How often would I have gathered your children together as a hen gathers her brood under her wings, and you were not willing!"* Here is a direct statement from Jesus about His work and desire and the response of the people in rejecting it. He called them, encouraged them, commanded them, chewed them out, and did everything He could to get them to listen to Him. However, Jesus says that it was their choice not to listen to Him. He wanted them to believe and receive the blessing of the kingdom of God on earth and for eternity; they rejected that. So it's clear that they had input in what happened to them.

- John 3:16: *"For God so loved the world, that he gave his only Son, that whoever believes in him should not perish but have eternal life."* The real key in this verse is the word "whoever." Jesus came and died for the sins of the whole world, and those who believe in Him experience the benefits of that death. To Arminians, the "whoever" is an open-ended statement that allows anyone to come into the kingdom. If they do not, then that is their choice. God calls, but we must respond.

- Acts 13:46: *"And Paul and Barnabas spoke out boldly, saying, 'It was necessary that the word of God be spoken*

*first to you. Since you thrust it aside and judge yourselves
unworthy of eternal life, behold, we are turning to the
Gentiles.* '" In Paul's words, it is not the fault of God that
the people of the synagogue in Pisidian Antioch didn't
receive the message that Paul and Barnabas brought to
them. It was their own fault that they rejected the message.
They judged *themselves* unworthy of eternal life. God
didn't judge them unworthy; they judged themselves
unworthy.

Conditional Security[28]

This is the part of Arminianism that causes a lot of trouble for
people.[29] Just like Calvinism had one point that a lot of Calvinists
are uncomfortable with (limited atonement), Conditional Security
is one that many Arminians squirm a little over. Arminius himself
left the question open of whether a true and saving faith could
ultimately fall away.[30] Some Free Will Baptists have held to
Calvinism's Perseverance of the Saints, though most Arminians

---

[28] Ibid., 186–187; Allen and Lemke, *Whosoever Will*, 163–190.
[29] This point is actually why the acrostic LILAC works better than DAISY. In
the caricature of Arminian theology that some people teach, the daisy is used
because people pick petals off the daisy, saying, "He loves me...He loves me
not..." This is not fair, as we shall see.
[30] Olson, *Arminian Theology*, 187.

side with the Remonstrants and Wesley and deny this. Instead, they hold that total apostasy[31] is a possibility for true believers.

For many Arminians, though, God's gifting of libertarian free will affects this point as well. God is good, and in His goodness God has given each person the freedom to choose for themselves where they go in life. This freedom, while seen as a good thing, can lead people to bad places, including sin. Since God is good, He desires genuine relationships with His worshippers. Because He desires genuine relationships, He allows libertarian freedom to trust Christ. This goodness and desire for genuine relationship, which leads to free will, means that the believer is left with the decision every day of whether to continue to trust Christ and pursue the relationship. Every person chooses whether they are a Christian, and that decision can be renounced.[32]

A further question is what happens when a person renounces their faith in Christ. While there are some who would maintain that a person who has left the faith is still a child of God and still heaven-bound, these people are among the minority.[33] Far more say that

---

[31] This is called apostasy, "A biblical concept that generally refers to those who fall away from belief in God." Grenz, Guretzki, and Nordling, *Pocket Dictionary of Theological Terms*, 14. This is a genuine difference between classical Arminians and Calvinists, because Arminians believe a genuine Christian can indeed do this.

[32] Forlines, *Classical Arminianism*, 314–324.

[33] Ibid, 306-313

God saves those who trust Christ, and if a person no longer trusts Christ, then they are once again under the wrath of God and once again in danger of the fires of hell. (John 15:1-6)

For Arminians of this type (which are the vast majority), the person who commits apostasy loses their salvation with their faith. That is, their security in Christ is guaranteed only as long as they persevere in the faith; their perseverance is their responsibility and is no guarantee. If a person fails to persevere in faith in Christ until death, their salvation may well be lost.

The Scriptures are clear in places about warning those who are believers of the consequences of falling away from trusting Christ. The fallout from walking away from the Lord is scary, to say the least:

- John 15:6: *"If anyone does not abide in me he is thrown away like a branch and withers; and the branches are gathered, thrown into the fire, and burned."* The person who does not "abide" in Christ is one who was with him (note in 15:2 Jesus describes the branch as "in Me") and then falls away from Christ. This person is thrown into the fire and burned, which is a picture of hell. So failing to continue to trust Christ severs a person from the blessings of Christ, including the blessing of heaven at the end of life.

- Romans 8:13: *"For if you live according to the flesh you will die, but if by the Spirit you put to death the deeds of the body, you will live."* Paul is addressing Christians in this section of Romans, reminding them that their conduct and faith still matter. If they walk by the Spirit (a picture of trusting Christ), they will have eternal life. If they instead return to the world, they will die, and that means eternal death. Our security in Christ is conditioned upon our continuance in the faith.

- 1 Corinthians 9:24–27: *"Do you not know that in a race all the runners run, but only one receives the prize? So run that you may obtain it. Every athlete exercises self-control in all things. They do it to receive a perishable wreath, but we an imperishable. So I do not run aimlessly; I do not box as one beating the air. But I discipline my body and keep it under control, lest after preaching to others I myself should be disqualified."* The Apostle Paul knew that even though He was a believer in Christ, he could still be disqualified if he failed to finish the race well. There was no guarantee that he would persevere until the end, which is why he focused on self-discipline and on keeping his faith strong.

The disqualification in mind is an eternal disqualification, and the wreath is a representation of eternal life.

- Galatians 5:4-6: "*You are severed from Christ, you who would be justified by the law; you have fallen away from grace. For through the Spirit, by faith, we ourselves eagerly wait for the hope of righteousness. For in Christ Jesus neither circumcision nor uncircumcision counts for anything, but only faith working through love.*" Clearly Paul is talking to those who are attached to Christ. They are connected to Him, but if they then stop trusting Christ and instead seek to be right in God's eyes through their own works, they will fall from that state of grace and be severed from Christ and from his benefits. This means that justification can be lost.

- Hebrews 3:12–14: "*Take care, brothers, lest there be in any of you an evil, unbelieving heart, leading you to fall away from the living God. But exhort one another every day, as long as it is called "today," that none of you may be hardened by the deceitfulness of sin. For we have come to share in Christ, if indeed we hold our original confidence firm to the end.*" Only those who don't harden their heart, and hold their original confidence (a synonym for faith) until the end of their life, keep their justification and receive final salvation. To share in Christ requires continuing in the faith, and those who fall away from Christ fall away from sharing in Him and in His kingdom.

Strengths and Concerns of Arminianism

Arminianism is easy to remember if we keep their flower front and center in our minds as we think about what they believe: LILAC. They hold to Limited Depravity, Individual Responsibility, Limitless Atonement, Arrestable Grace, and Conditional Security. The focus of Arminianism is upon the goodness of God, and because of that goodness Arminianism teaches that God desires genuine relationship that is authentic and not forced in any way.

Just as Calvinism has strengths and areas of concern, so does Arminianism. In fact, the concerns of Calvinism line up nicely with the strengths of Arminianism, and the strengths of Calvinism highlight many of the concerns of Arminianism. This makes a lot of sense because these two systems have dominated Protestant Christian thinking for 500 or so years and are tuned by those who believe in them to play up the weaknesses of the other.

Strengths

+ It protects God's justice and highlights His mercy. God has given to each person free will to choose to follow Him and Christ's sacrifice so that they can approach him without works to pay for their sins. He is still just because His standard of perfection is met, yet merciful because the Gospel message is open to all.

+ Assurance is, for most Arminians, easier to grasp because there is less focus on so-called "false conversions." If you trust Christ, then you can be assured of eternal life. (See below, however, for an accompanying concern.)

+ Arminians read many passages of Scripture in a very straightforward and simple manner. If it is written to believers, then for Arminians it means genuine believers. If it says they can fall away, then they can and that is bad. If God gives a command, then He gives the ability to obey that command, even the call to trust Christ.

+ Free will and honest relationship. Many statements in Scripture seem to point to human beings having significant moral decision-making power, including over eternal life. God's goodness brings free will, which in turn provides for honest relationship and not coercion.

+ Arminian theology is the dominant worldwide theology in Protestantism today. While Calvinism has a strong following in the USA, the rest of the world of Protestant Christianity is Arminian. Wesleyan Arminianism (in the form of Pentecostal denominations) and Anglican churches dominate much of southern Africa as well as Asia. In

Europe, Calvinism has few adherents (but then again, evangelical Christianity is pretty sparse there too).

Concerns

- It is difficult to see how we work together with God to accomplish salvation, and still maintain that we didn't work for our salvation. Though Arminian writers have wrestled with this problem and proposed answers, for many the answers are not convincing. We know salvation is not of works and is not of ourselves (Ephesians 2:8-9), and the Arminian idea of synergism is hard to put together with that.

- The sovereignty of God is sometimes diminished in Arminian theology.[34] God doesn't just seem to know the end, but to declare it in the sense of causing it. (Isaiah 46:10) This can potentially lead to bad steps in theology[35], which is dangerous.

---

[34] Arminians would certainly disagree, saying that God is the one who had the sovereign right to decide to allow us free will and set the conditions for eternal life. But the concerns remain nevertheless, especially with some of the texts of Scripture speaking not only of God's control of all things, but the fact that He does so above and beyond the choices of people.

[35] The big one that has received a lot of attention in the last ten years is called "Open Theism," which says that God doesn't know the future and therefore our decisions are really free decisions. Saying that God doesn't know the future throws a HUGE monkey wrench in so much of Scripture and must play reindeer games with a lot of verses, but it can become a "next step" theologically for some who really see free will as the cornerstone of their theology. For a

- While believers in Christ can have present assurance, their assurance can be lost because they cannot guarantee that they will continue to believe. If their salvation stands upon them continuing to believe, and they have libertarian free will to choose to believe or not at all times, then there is nothing saying that in the future that they couldn't stop believing and therefore lose their salvation. So in the end, assurance is very difficult to come by. Assurance about this moment is possible, but firm assurance about the future is not.

- While Arminian theology takes a lot of Scripture at face value, it seems that many times language about the deadness of human will, and our bondage to sin as unbelievers, isn't taken nearly as easily aboard. The same holds true for the idea of the security of the salvation of those who are saved. (Remember, though, that there are some Arminians who believe that salvation cannot be lost)

If you'd like to read more about Arminianism, there are also several good books that are helpful for understanding the system from their perspective:

---

response to Open Theism, I recommend Bruce A. Ware, *God's Lesser Glory: The Diminished God of Open Theism* (Downers Grove, IL: Crossway, 2000).

David L. Allen and Steve W. Lemke, eds., *Whosoever Will: A Biblical-Theological Critique of Five-Point Calvinism* (Nashville, TN; B&H Academic, 2010). Though the title sounds like it is an interaction with Calvinism, the reality is that it argues for Arminianism as an alternative.

F. Leroy Forlines, *Classical Arminianism*, ed. J. Matthew Pinson (Nashville, TN; Randall House Publications, 2011) This book sets out the basic tenets of Arminian theology in an easy-to-read manner. Though he can be a bit attacking at times, overall the book is a good read.

Dave Hunt and James White, *Debating Calvinism: Five Points, Two Views* (Colorado Springs, CO; Multnomah Books, 2004). This book is obviously not just Arminian, but is a helpful comparison and contrast of these two views by two firm supporters.

Roger E. Olson, *Against Calvinism* (Grand Rapids, MI; Zondervan, 2011).

Roger E. Olson, *Arminian Theology: Myths and Realities*, Fifth Printing. (Downers Grove, IL: IVP Academic, 2006). Much of the understanding of this section of the book is taken from this work by Olson. It is well-written and kind in its approach.

Robert E. Picirilli, *Grace, Faith, Free Will* (Nashville, TN; Randall House Publications, 2002). This book is promoted as a "contrasting views" book, but is decidedly Arminian in its approach.

Jerry L. Walls and Joseph R. Dongell, *Why I Am Not a Calvinist* (Downers Grove, IL; IVP Books, 2004).

There are plenty of people who prefer LILACs in their garden to TULIPs, but there are still a lot of concerns. Yes, Arminians focus on the goodness of God, and that's good. But Calvinists focus on the greatness of God, and that's great! Many people, having read both systems and after understanding how the proponents of each think and what they value, are left with confusion and even with frustration because each has good points but neither has freedom from significant concerns.

So what are we to do? Some will throw up their hands and try to opt out,[36] but whether they know it or not they *will* adopt a system of some kind to explain how salvation works. Having looked at the two most dominant systems in Christian thought for the past 500 years, it's now our task to take a moment to consider systems in general, and the limits of systems, before approaching the problem from a different angle.

---

[36] These folks are the theological hipsters of the church, but you've probably never heard of them or what they believe.

Questions for Individual Thought and Group Discussion:

1. Which letter of LILAC do you think has the best evidence? Why is it strong?

2. Which letter of LILAC do you think has the most challenges? What are its weaknesses?

3. What do you think of Arminianism's central idea of God's goodness? Do you think that there is enough evidence in Scripture to make this the central idea of God in salvation? Why or why not?

4. Before starting this study, would you have considered yourself an Arminian? Would you now? Why or why not?

5. Does Limitless Atonement cheapen the grace of God? Does it undermine the justice of God in sending people to hell whose sins are paid for?

6. If you're not an Arminian, which point can you respect the most? If you are, which point do you think is most difficult for non-Arminians to appreciate?

Chapter 4: The Limits of Our Flower Boxes

At this point, having looked at the overwhelmingly dominant systems of salvation in the Christian church today, it is worthwhile to take a moment to assess where we are in the discussion. This has been a 500-year stalemate, so maybe it is time to see if there is a different approach to the problem or if we have placed unfair expectations on the task at hand. Some Christians expect their system of theology to be perfect. It's not possible; only Jesus is perfect! Using our analogy of a flower bed, there is no perfect flower. Some have more brilliant colors, some smell wonderfully,[1] some are drought resistant, and some are easy to grow. All have strengths and weaknesses.

We must recognize that all systems of theology have their limitations as well; this is every bit as true for Calvinism and Arminianism as for any other system dealing with any other issue in theology. If the issue was crystal clear, there would be nothing to discuss! These limitations come, at the end of the day, to limits within each system and to systems in general. Anyone claiming that their system has every answer and no questions or challenges

---

[1] And some smell like corpses. Don't believe me? Check it out: Wikipedia contributors, "Rafflesia," *Wikipedia, the free encyclopedia* (Wikimedia Foundation, Inc., June 12, 2012), http://en.wikipedia.org/w/index.php?title=Rafflesia&oldid=496980333. Online. (accessed June 15, 2012).

either hasn't thought through their system very well or is living in a fantasy world. In fact, this is a good way to tell if you're talking to someone about salvation who is honest and thoughtful: anyone who argues that their understanding is flawless and airtight is in need of a checkup from the neck up, while those who can acknowledge the weaknesses and flaws of their system and talk about them is probably good to go.

All systems have limitations, and all systems have weaknesses. Mature believers recognize this and the limits and weaknesses of the system that they ascribe to, as well as its strengths. Certainly we would expect that they would think that the strengths are stronger and the concerns less alarming than those of other systems, but we must be honest with one another about this issue.

At this point it is worth considering a quote from Roger Olson about how our various systems work and their limits.

> *"The point here is that both sides (and perhaps all significant theological systems) involve mystery, and in making their theological systems perfectly intelligible, mystery is a problem. Ironically, both sides tend to point out the other's weakness in appealing to mystery without acknowledging their own. Both point to the speck in the other's eye*

while ignoring the equally large speck (beam?) in
their own! Thus it appears that people are not
Calvinists or Arminians because one side has
proven itself right, but because these people can
find one set of mysteries (or problems) easier to live
with than the other. Of course, adherents of both
also point to supporting Scriptures and experiences
(such as being grasped by God apart from an
awareness of choice). [2]

Neither side can claim a complete or total victory; neither side has all of the evidence or all of the points in their favor. If one had all of the positives and none of the negatives, then there would be no debate. However, it is clear that both have significant strengths while encountering significant concerns.

This is where the discussion gets a bit tricky, because to truly get to the bottom of this debate we actually need to look past the issue at hand to the issue *behind* the issue. We might think that the issue is simply seen in how we handle the texts, but our understanding of God has more to it than that. If we could purely look at the text without any previous understanding of God and build our theology from the text of Scripture itself in a total vacuum, then we could claim to be pure biblical theologians. However, that is just not

---

[2] Olson, *Arminian Theology*, 72.

possible in reality. In reality there are many influences on our understanding of the text of Scripture and we must consider them as we study.

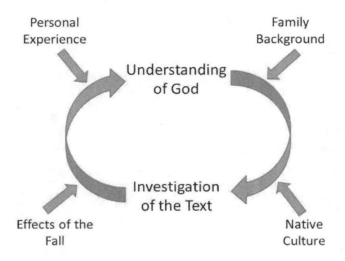

These different influences along with an investigation of the text lead us to an overarching picture of who God is and what He is like. Our own personal experience might affect our understanding; for instance, if our earthly father was loving and kind to us it may influence us to see God as fundamentally loving and kind. If our culture values power and control our view of God might be influenced to see Him as powerful. If our family has a long history in the Assemblies of God or the Presbyterian Church in America it may well influence how we see God's attributes.

While we all may agree that our biggest contributor to understanding God should be the text of Scripture, there is no denying that there are also other influences. Those influences color how we view God, and how we view God in turn impacts how we understand the biblical text. This cycle of understanding is important to grasp, because at some point we have enough information and background and understanding to realize that our fundamental view of who God is becomes as much a driving force in our view of Scripture as the other way around.

> *Contrary to popular belief, then, the true divide at the heart of the Calvinist-Arminian split is not predestination versus free will but the guiding picture of God: he is primarily viewed as either (1) majestic, powerful, and controlling or (2) loving, good, and merciful. Once the picture…is established, seemingly contrary aspects fade into the background, are set aside as "obscure" or are artificially made to fit the system. Neither side absolutely denies the truth of the other's perspective, but each qualifies the attributes of God that are preeminent in the other's perspective. God's goodness is qualified by his greatness in*

Calvinism, and God's greatness is qualified by his goodness in Arminianism."[3]

Both of these sides have their Scriptural points, and both, as Olson says, end up appealing to mystery to handle the conflicts that arise when passages that don't fit the overriding vision for who God is surface. Within Calvinism, the central understanding is the *glory* of God; within Arminianism, it is the *goodness* of God. As Olson points out, Calvinists uphold God's goodness and Arminians agree that God is sovereign, but these are not the center around which they build their understanding of God and of salvation.

So which is more central to who God is? Is God's glory the center of our understanding of God? Is the most fundamental aspect of God's character His goodness? In many ways, the answer that we choose for that question tells us more about our picture of who God is at a fundamental level than it does about which system is more "correct" in its understanding of who God is. It shows us the lens through which we approach God. That alone is a helpful piece of information to have because it lets us know what our approach is to God.

While Calvinism agrees that God is good and Arminianism says that God is in control, both have to qualify those statements and

---

[3] Ibid., 73.

defend them against people who say that the respective system doesn't cut it with that issue. In other words, non-Calvinists have a hard time with agreeing that Calvinism as a system upholds the goodness of God. Likewise, Calvinists argue that Arminians devalue the greatness of God by downplaying His sovereign control over His creation. So the question remains, which reigns supreme? Is God good or is He great?

The Scripture teaches both and does not hold them in tension but in unison. They don't need reconciliation because as the famous saying goes, you don't have to reconcile friends! Scripture doesn't really qualify God's goodness in light of His greatness; likewise, the Bible never holds God's greatness at the mercy of His goodness. Instead, God's greatness comes because of His goodness and His goodness is only truly good because of His greatness. Accepting that premise isn't necessarily all that hard (and I would expect that most Calvinists and Arminians would agree with it), but building a system of understanding of salvation that upholds both without qualification is a bit trickier.

What if we had a theological system that attempted to untie the Gordian knot[4] and do just that? What if there was another system

---

[4] The "Gordian knot" is an ancient Greek myth about a peasant named Gordius who became king of Phrygia and tied his cart to a pole by means of an incredibly intricate knot. An oracle predicted that the knot would be untied by the future king of Asia, and it sat unsolved despite the efforts of many. The knot

that upheld the glorious greatness and sovereignty of God while at the same time grasped His goodness in seeking genuine relationship through creaturely freedom? If we could find that type of system it would indeed be a Refreshing Grace that we could all use! That system would have to attempt to uphold both without qualification of any attribute of God. It would certainly have its limitations as all systems do, and would likely have to remember that no system is perfect. That said, perhaps in this system we would find that the central motif would be...

The *greatness* and *goodness* of God are found upheld in His *grace*.

Questions for Individual Thought and Group Discussion:

1. Since there is no such thing as a perfect system, should we abandon our search to find a system to understand salvation?

---

was not solved until Alexander the Great came and, after looking the knot over carefully, became frustrated and cut through it with his sword. The phrase, then, refers to a seemingly unsolvable problem that can only be solved by thinking "outside the box" and not accepting the limitations of the system.

2. What influences you as you approach the text of Scripture? What is your biggest influence outside of the text itself, and what kind of biases does that influence make you prone to?

3. Do you agree with the idea that, at least in some measure, we adopt a system not because it is better but because it fits our picture of God more easily? If so, is this a good approach? Should our feelings about who God should be determine how we understand who He actually is?

Chapter 5: Molinism-Coming Up ROSES

Classical Calvinism has as its central interpretive motif the glory of
God, and because of His glory He controls all that comes to pass.
Arminianism, by contrast, has as its central interpretive motif the
goodness of God, and because of His goodness God in prevenient
grace allows humans to have libertarian free will and choice to
make decisions. Roger Olson has postulated that there is no
middle ground between them;[1] in the old idiom, "Oh, East is East,
and West is West, and never the twain shall meet."[2]

There is another system available for understanding the
intersection of divine control and human free will than those
offered by Calvinism and Arminianism. That viewpoint is known
as Molinism, which is named after the 16th century theologian Luis
de Molina.[3] It has been explained thoroughly in the modern
writings of William Lane Craig.[4] Molinism hasn't been nearly as

---

[1] Olson, *Arminian Theology*, 61–77.
[2] Rudyard Kipling, "The Ballad of East and West"
[3] Interestingly, the system can probably be traced back to Balthasar Hubmaier,
though perhaps "Molinism" rolls off the tongue more readily than
"Hubmaierism" or something similar.
[4] Some of Craig's works that are worth considering are William Lane Craig, *The
Only Wise God: The Compatibility of Divine Foreknowledge & Human
Freedom* (Eugene, OR: Wipf & Stock Publishers, 2000). and *Brill's Studies in
Intellectual History, Divine Foreknowledge and Human Freedom: The
Coherence of Theism: Omniscience* (Leiden: Brill Academic Publishers, 2005)
among the many. It is also very wise to look to the writings of Alvin Plantinga,
whose book *God, Freedom, and Evil* (Grand Rapids, MI: William B. Eerdmans

popular in American churches because there are so many more books and lectures from Calvinists and Arminians; the great revival preachers of our country's past like Jonathan Edwards and Billy Graham have taken Calvinism and Arminianism as their understanding of God.

That said, Molinism is a viable and helpful alternative for those who have a hard time accepting either Calvinism or Arminianism. Molinism isn't a "middle ground"; it is an entirely different way to look at the problem of God's control and human free will. Perhaps the best recent treatment of this viewpoint comes from Kenneth Keathley.[5] Keathley begins his take on this challenge by asking some significant questions that many Christians find valid:

> What shall a Christian do who is convinced of
> certain central tenets of Calvinism but not its
> corollaries? Specifically, what if I am convinced
> that God elects individuals to salvation but I am
> also compelled by the evidence of Scripture to

Publishing Company, 1978) is an incredible defense of a wholly good, sovereign, omnipotent, omnibenevolent God allowing creaturely freedom and evil in the world while maintaining his character. With both of these guys, be forewarned that if you are brave enough to crack their books you will definitely be challenged and your brain will hurt. Look up Craig on YouTube and watch some of his videos explaining philosophy and God and you'll get my drift.
[5] Kenneth Keathley, *Salvation and Sovereignty: A Molinist Approach* (Nashville, TN; B&H Academic, 2010). This discussion will be primarily based on Keathley's book, with a few significant tweaks and nuances.

reject the notion that Christ died only for the elect?
What if I am also convinced that the Calvinist
doctrine of irresistible grace—that God gives saving
grace only to the elect while withholding it from
others—has little or no biblical foundation?[6]

A Christian who finds themselves in this dilemma of attempting to
uphold both sides of this debate might often call themselves a
"Calminian", i.e. a half-Calvinist half-Arminian hybrid. However,
once understood it is likely better that they embrace the system
known as Molinism, for in it the student of Scripture finds the
ability to uphold both God's sovereignty that is so entwined in
Scripture and the ability and responsibility of people to make free
choices that is also affirmed there. They get a two for one deal!

Molinism holds to a Calvinist view of God's sovereignty, for in the
Calvinist model of God's greatness Molinism finds the best
biblical evidence. God is in control of all things, and He is
completely sovereign. Molinism also holds to a modified
Arminian view of human freedom, again because the Scripture
affirms it. Our decisions are, at critical times, free decisions within
Molinism. This causes Molinism to be attacked by both Calvinism
(as Arminian) and Arminianism (as Calvinistic)!

---

[6] Ibid., 1.

Molinism's garden is a bit different than Arminianism's or Calvinism's. Though Calvinism's TULIPs were planted completely by God, and Arminianism's LILACs were planted by us, in Molinism God creates the world in which we choose of our free will to plant the ROSES in exactly the way that God desires. He is both in complete control of history and grants us free will in planting ROSES. The center of Molinism is not the greatness or goodness of God, but the wisdom of God in combining those two without violating either.

The tension of Scripture and system is reconciled through the means of God's *middle knowledge*. Because this idea is not very well understood in Christian circles today, we can't jump right in to the ROSES of Molinism. Instead we have to start by "tilling the soil" of our flower box so to speak by understanding what God knows and how He knows it, and from there we need to change our understanding of how God controls history.

Middle Knowledge: the heart of Molinism[7]

Molinism's foundation rests on describing and defining what God knows and how He knows it. It's all about God's wisdom! After we unpack the way God knows and what God knows, we have to consider how He uses that knowledge, especially how He uses His

---

[7] Ibid., 16–41.

knowledge in control over history and creation. God controls creation by means of His wisdom in light of His full knowledge of all possible events and actions and outcomes in the universe, not merely His sovereign will. Therefore *how* God knows and *what* God knows are very important.

The big issue to keep in mind here is grasping God's knowledge. Molinism describes God's knowledge according to three "moments." We must be very careful not to think of them as points in time but as points in logical order. They are "instants" in some way because they aren't really time-bound. That said, the term "moment" works as well as any other so we will use it. These three moments can be described simply in terms of "could," "would," and "will."[8]

---

[8] Chart is from Ibid., 17.

The Three Moments of Molinism in Terms of "Could," "Would," and "Will": God uses His omniscience to perfectly accomplish His will		
1st Moment: God's Natural Knowledge	"Could": Everything that could happen	God knows all possibilities
2nd Moment: God's Middle Knowledge	"Would": Everything that would happen	God knows which possibilities are feasible
Between 2nd & 3rd moment: God freely and sovereignly chooses this particular world from the infinite number of feasible possibilities.		
3rd Moment: God's Free Knowledge	"Will": Everything that will happen	God exhaustively knows all things.

These "moments" must be unpacked and understood as they progress and describe how God works all things together in His wisdom. First, God's *natural knowledge* describes God's knowledge of all possibilities. He knows everything that could happen. He knows every possible scenario and situation in any created world imaginable. He knows what the world would be like if He had decided to create Middle Earth[9] instead of this world, or what the world would look like without the wheel ever being invented. He knows every detail about every world He could possibly have made. There is a staggeringly large number of theoretically possible worlds, and God knows them all perfectly. Because He is all-knowing, He knows all possibilities as a natural part of His being; therefore this knowledge is called His *natural knowledge.* Naturally, God knows every conceivable scenario in any possible world. That's a lot of knowledge!

From the natural knowledge of God we must skip the second "moment" and move to the third before coming back to the second. (We shall see why as they are explained) The third moment is known as God's *free knowledge* because it relates to the world that He actually did choose to freely create. Of all of the possible worlds that He could have chosen to create, He was not required to create any of them. He could have chosen to create nothing, or a world without cars, or a world where the Germans won WWII, or a world where lions were vegetarians. He could have chosen to create a world where people have no choice in anything at any

---

[9] For non-nerds, this is what the world in the Lord of the Rings series of books and movies is called. And I freely admit that it would be way more awesome.

time, or a world in which He chose not to step in and save anyone and let everyone do whatever they wanted at any time. Instead of any of those choices or a million billion others, God chose of His own will to create the world that we actually inhabit.[10] He is in complete, sovereign control of that choice and no one and nothing forced God to create the world we live in. That means this choice was free, and that's why we call this God's *free knowledge*. He freely chose to create this world, knowing everything about it.

The problem so far is that God chose to create a world with creatures capable of making moral decisions.[11] In other words, His decision was to create a world that He is in charge of in which our decisions actually matter. How can He control history while still allowing us to have freedom to make decisions? This is the classic argument between Calvinism and Arminianism. Arminianism holds up God's goodness and because of that goodness it upholds

---

[10] I suppose we could ask the question at this point about why God chose to create *this* world rather than some other world, and it's a fair question. There are good answers, but to dive into them requires us to leave the realm of theology and head into the realm of philosophy, which is beyond our purpose. Read the book suggestions at the end of the chapter for some discussion on this question.
[11] For the moment we must assume and agree with the Arminian idea that humans have some significant moral ability and free will. Even some Calvinists would agree with that in a limited sense, so this is no big stretch.

free will. Calvinism upholds God's sovereign control and complete care for creation and because of that denies a libertarian free will.[12]

This is where Molinism gets a little tricky, but also a whole bunch of awesome. Rather than try to qualify God's greatness by His goodness, or His goodness by His greatness, Molinism looks at the second "moment" of God's knowledge as the point in which His goodness is brought to the front by His greatness in His grace. This second moment is where the rubber meets the road, as God's wisdom takes center stage. This is God's *middle knowledge* because it comes in the middle of His natural and free knowledge.

Middle Knowledge can be described as God not only knowing what *could* happen and what *will* happen, but what would happen *if.* God possesses counter-factual knowledge, which means that He knows what would happen if things had been different. For example, He knows what would have happened if He had spared the Canaanites from destruction, or what Napoleon would have done had he won the battle of Waterloo. He knows how your life would be different if you had never picked up this book. He knows what any free agent would do in any situation, not because

---

[12] This is not always 100% the case, as noted above. Some American Calvinists and more European Calvinists allow for some limited free will in their understanding of God, though the majority does not. The classic Calvinism described earlier doesn't much allow for it, and in allowing it into their system these theologians modify or soften their understanding of Calvinism. This is fine, though not always completely consistent.

the circumstances caused the choice, but because He knows their hearts perfectly and knows that this is how a free creature who He knows perfectly and completely would have chosen. Therefore, God knows if He sets up a situation, what would occur because of that situation and because of a person's own free choices in that situation. He knows not only what creatures *could* do, nor only what they *will* do, but what they *would* do in any given situation He could possibly put them in.

Here's where the idea gets crazy: He knows all these potentials to the ends of the history of the earth. He knows how a change in one decision in one person's life would affect not only them, but those who interact with them and the changes that decision would make in their life, as well as the ripples it would cause throughout history.[13] God knows every decision made by every person throughout history and how the world would be different if one person made one decision differently. Multiply that by the thousands of decisions made by billions of people every day for

---

[13] For anyone raised in the 80's, think of the television show "Quantum Leap." In that show, by changing something in the time he is in Sam (the show's protagonist) changes the course of history going forward. Al (Sam's holographic sidekick) had a handheld computer named Ziggy that would tell them when they changed something in history that a desired (or not desired) outcome would happen. That's counterfactual knowledge, though not exhaustive or perfect like God's really is. And seriously, if you never watched the show, go find it on Netflix. You'll thank me.

the number of years of history and your brain will start to grasp the magnitude of God's knowledge!

Therefore, Middle knowledge says that God combines human free will and God's total control of creation in this manner:

1. God knows exactly who His elect are and, of all of the possible worlds that He could have created, which worlds among those where His elect will come to faith in Christ.

2. Having set up the condition of faith alone in Christ alone for eternal life, and desiring authentic relationship with His creation, God knows out of the possible worlds He could create where His elect actually do come to faith in Christ, which possible worlds will accomplish His desired ends by means of truly free decisions.

3. By knowing His creation perfectly and completely, God has the ability to know exactly what every creature *will* do in any given situation and with any given set of motivation, and can therefore choose to create the world in which their meaningful decisions carry out His sovereign will without having to coerce them to choose what He wants.

4. Therefore, between "moments" 2 and 3 in the table above, God chooses to actually create the world that carries out His truly sovereign plan using truly free decisions. God freely determines to determine freely.

Of course, this entire system only holds any water if Scripture does uphold the fact that God has middle knowledge. Thankfully, Scripture shows us that God does indeed have counterfactual knowledge, giving us strong evidence for middle knowledge as Molinism describes it. While there are several places we could look to see that God has this kind of knowledge, the story of David in 1 Samuel 23:6-14 shows it very clearly:

> *"When Abiathar the son of Ahimelech had fled to David to Keilah, he had come down with an ephod in his hand. Now it was told Saul that David had come to Keilah. And Saul said, "God has given him into my hand, for he has shut himself in by entering a town that has gates and bars." And Saul summoned all the people to war, to go down to Keilah, to besiege David and his men. David knew that Saul was plotting harm against him. And he said to Abiathar the priest, "Bring the ephod here." Then David said, "O LORD, the God of Israel, your servant has surely heard that Saul seeks to come to Keilah, to destroy the city on my account. Will the men of Keilah surrender me into his hand? Will Saul come down, as your servant has heard? O LORD, the God of Israel, please tell your servant."*

And the LORD said, "He will come down." Then
David said, "Will the men of Keilah surrender me
and my men into the hand of Saul?" And the LORD
said, "They will surrender you." Then David and
his men, who were about six hundred, arose and
departed from Keilah, and they went wherever they
could go. When Saul was told that David had
escaped from Keilah, he gave up the expedition.
And David remained in the strongholds in the
wilderness, in the hill country of the wilderness of
Ziph. And Saul sought him every day, but God did
not give him into his hand."

David uses an ephod to inquire of the Lord whether Saul would
attack Keilah where David was. The ephod was a device that the
priests used to hear from God and determine His will, and so it was
a way for the priests to communicate with God. David really
wanted to know whether the men of Keilah would deliver David
over to Saul. So David asks God *if* Saul was going to come, and *if*
that happened whether the men of Keilah would be loyal to Saul.
He is asking God about the future.

God told him the future, and that's where it gets interesting. God
tells David that Saul *will* come, and that the men of Keilah *will*
turn David over to him. David uses that information to good effect

to flee the city so that the predictions do not in fact come true. So in reality, God was not telling David what would actually come to pass, but what would happen *if* David stayed in Keilah! What the device had told David was not simple foreknowledge of what definitely will happen, but counter-factual knowledge of what would happen if. God was letting David know that if he were to remain in Keilah then Saul would come after him; from there, God said that if Saul were to come after David then the men of Keilah would deliver him over to Saul. The answers given by the ephod were correct answers even though the events did not come to pass, since the answers were indicative of what would happen under certain circumstances. The Scriptures show us that God has counterfactual knowledge![14]

So the system of Molinism is coherent and, more importantly, there is biblical evidence that God does indeed possess middle knowledge. Obviously, Molinism does not get off scot-free in the problem department. All theologies have their issues! However, it seems to handle the problems of Calvinism and Arminianism in biblically sound ways and can help us reconcile God's sovereign control over history with the free decisions of people in history. How it does so remains to be seen.

---

[14] Craig, *The Only Wise God*, 131–138.

The System: A Nicer Smelling Flower

Since Calvinism and Arminianism have their own acrostic,
Molinism can't be left out of the flowerbox! Molinism prefers to
grow ROSES to TULIPs or LILACs. The only challenge with the
acrostic (and an unfortunate one) is that to make it spell a pretty
flower, the points are in slightly different order than Calvinism or
Arminianism. Now that we've seen it twice, though, it shouldn't be
too hard to keep up with the points in a different order. Molinists
believe that the Scriptures teach **R**adical Depravity, **O**vercoming
Grace, **S**age Election, **E**ternal Security, and **S**ingular Redemption.

When studying them, we will find that there are many elements
present that sound like Calvinism or Arminianism. That's the
whole point! As Norm Geisler says, "For the Christian, the starting
point in any analysis of sovereignty and free will must be the
Scriptures, and they clearly affirm that both are true—sometimes
even in the same verse."[15] Rather than trying to be a "middle
ground," though, Molinism tries to take a very different approach
that upholds the best elements of both systems while attempting to

---

[15] Norman L. Geisler, *Chosen But Free: A Balanced View of God's Sovereignty and Free Will*, 3rd ed. (Minneapolis, MN: Bethany House Publishers, 2010), 133. Geisler does not believe in Molinism but in Thomism, but his quotation is helpful here nevertheless. Describing Thomism as a system is beyond the scope of this work, though the difference with Molinism lies in its understanding of how God's grace and free will relate.

minimize the concerns of each. God is sovereign *and* we have libertarian free will, as ROSES shows.

Radical Depravity[16]

Much like Calvinism, Molinism says that humans are completely depraved. Remember, Arminianism agrees as well but qualifies what total depravity means. So does Molinism, but in a different way than Arminianism. We are in bondage to sin (John 8:34) and yet we are not completely morally corrupt. It's not hard to see that we're not utterly depraved, because humans exhibit a range of moral behaviors, from commendable to absolutely abominable. (Luke 12:46-48; Acts 10:22) In their fallen state humans do good things too, even things that they think will please God. (Matthew 7:21-23) Even though unbelieving humans *can* exhibit moral good, it does not mean that anything they do can earn their place with God. (Isaiah 64:6) The best person in history, in their natural state, is unable to respond to God. (1 Corinthians 2:14) This sounds very Calvinist!

However, within the Molinist understanding of depravity we are still left with some limited ability to make choices. Remember that in Arminian theology we have *libertarian free will*,[17] meaning the

---

[16] Keathley, *Salvation and Sovereignty*, 63–100.

[17] Remember, this has nothing to do with politics, but the idea is the same in that people have the ability to decide for themselves.

choices that we make are always our own and always freely made without outside control. This is called *hard libertarianism* because we always have it; it's hard and fast with no exceptions. Calvinists generally believe in *determinism*, which says that we choose only within our nature. Since our nature is depraved, we would never choose God and never can make a truly free decision. Molinism, though, seeks a different understanding of depravity and free will.

Molinism doesn't hold to either high Calvinism's determinism[18] or Arminianism's hard libertarianism. Our depravity does not remove all choice, but instead limits the range of available choices to a limited set. We can choose freely within a limited set of possibilities. This is called *soft libertarian free will*. We have choices, but not to make any choice whatsoever at all times.

Think about it from the perspective of a person who is faced with the choice to marry someone. If they choose to marry that person, it limits their ability in the future in that they can't then marry someone else.[19] Their one choice sets them up for limits in their potentials in the future. In another example, consider a young woman who finds a wallet with an ID and a wad of cash in it. If she finds the owner and gives it back it will set her down one path,

---

[18] Determinism is the idea that God causes all that comes to pass. (Grenz, Guretzki, and Nordling, *Pocket Dictionary of Theological Terms*, 38) Therefore, human decisions are determined by God rather than free will.

[19] We're talking biblically here; don't push the analogy by talking polygamy or divorce and remarriage.

but if she keeps the cash and throws the ID and wallet away it will take her down another. When a person enlists in the military, they limit their available choices for some significant time.

There are many times when our previous choices make us bound to a course of action where in some sense we have no functional freedom to choose differently after we've made the first choice. At the Diet of Worms (which sounds like a way to gross out girls but is actually an assembly of Catholic bishops in Worms, Germany, in 1521), Martin Luther was commanded to take back his criticism of the Roman Catholic Church; he famously said, "I am bound by the Scriptures I have quoted and my conscience is captive to the Word of God."[20] His previous decision to trust Christ and embrace salvation by faith alone in Christ alone made it impossible for him to go back; his first decision limited his other decisions, though that first one was his to make.

So within Molinism we have complete and utter sinfulness of people, but some limited ability to make decisions. The verses mentioned within Calvinism's section on total depravity and Arminianism's section on Limited Depravity both apply here, and don't need to be repeated. They're both true, and taken together they say that we are totally depraved but we are also left with some

---

[20] George W. Forell, *Luther's Works, Volume 32: Career of the Reformer II*, ed. Helmut T. Lehman (Minneapolis: Fortress Press, 1958), 112.

significant decision making ability at key moments. This is nowhere more clearly seen than in Luke 7:29-30 which was discussed in Arminianism's "Arrestable Grace":

> "*(When all the people heard this, and the tax collectors too, they declared God just, having been baptized with the baptism of John, but the Pharisees and the lawyers rejected the purpose of God for themselves, not having been baptized by him.)*"

The Pharisees in verse 30 did not accept John's baptism, and so when they heard the Gospel presented by Jesus they rejected it. They had the decision to make and they made it negatively. The people, along with the tax collectors, chose the opposite way because of the choice they had previously made to accept John's baptism. So the previous choice was free, but this choice was in a large sense caused by that previous one.

So we are radically depraved, for all the reasons embraced by Calvinism. The depravity that we have does taint our ability to make choices, and we do not always have freedom of will. At key moments, though, God ensures that our ability to choose is significant and we can indeed choose to do the right thing or the wrong thing. This is true for most choices, but the time of the presentation of the gospel is a special event that deserves special consideration.[21] Because it is so unique as a decision and as an event, God uses overcoming grace to save us in a way that is all of God and still involves free will.

Overcoming Grace[22]

This model seeks to keep salvation all of God (as in Calvinism), and yet be resistible (as in Arminianism). Whereas Calvinism's grace is *irresistible* and Arminianism's grace is *arrestable*, in Molinism grace is *overcoming* in that God's grace overcomes our radical depravity to save us from ourselves.

This is done with the maxim "salvation is all of grace, and damnation is all of sin."[23] In this understanding, salvation is entirely the work of God in someone's life; they have no part in salvation, only accepting it by not resisting God's work in their heart. (Ephesians 2:8-9) If they resist, then their failure to trust Christ is because of their own resistance and they are responsible for their own damnation. (Acts 13:46) God is wholly responsible for salvation and our decision to trust Him, but it is our responsibility not to resist His work in our lives to bring us to faith in Jesus and therefore to salvation.

---

[21] Keathley, *Salvation and Sovereignty*, 88.
[22] Ibid., 101–137.
[23] Ibid., 103.

This is understood through an "ambulatory model" of salvation.[24] Much like an ambulance carries someone to the hospital without their needing to help the ambulance along, the Spirit carries sinners to Christ. (Philippians 1:28-29) However, just like a patient can refuse to accept transport to the hospital, so a sinner can refuse to allow Christ to save them. (John 12:48) So the "ambulatory" model is named because it works like an ambulance bringing a patient to the hospital. When they get to the hospital they've done nothing that earns them a bit of credit, but they can refuse to be transported and therefore never get to the hospital at all.

In this model, "faith" is allowing God to do what He desires to do in our lives. Trust is seen as accepting the calling of God upon us to let Him save us. It is entirely passive; we do nothing. What we "do" is actually something we *don't* do, which is reject the drawing and calling of the Spirit. His job is to convict us of sin, righteousness, and judgment, and He does that well. (John 16:8) If we don't fight Him, then He works in our hearts to trust Christ and rebirths us as Christians. (John 3:3-8) Therefore, salvation is 100% of God's doing, in which we receive no merit or do no work. At the same time, condemnation is 100% of our doing because if we resist God then we are accountable for that.

---

[24] Ibid., 104–105.

This is seen well in Jesus' parable of the wedding feast in Matthew 22:1-7:

> *"And again Jesus spoke to them in parables, saying,*
> *"The kingdom of heaven may be compared to a king*
> *who gave a wedding feast for his son, and sent his*
> *servants to call those who were invited to the*
> *wedding feast, but they would not come. Again he*
> *sent other servants, saying, 'Tell those who are*
> *invited, "See, I have prepared my dinner, my oxen*
> *and my fat calves have been slaughtered, and*
> *everything is ready. Come to the wedding feast." '*
> *But they paid no attention and went off, one to his*
> *farm, another to his business, while the rest seized*
> *his servants, treated them shamefully, and killed*
> *them. The king was angry, and he sent his troops*
> *and destroyed those murderers and burned their*
> *city."*

It's not wise to push the interpretation of parables too far, and within this we must realize that the key with parables is to keep the main point firmly in mind.[25] The main point in this particular parable is that many people were invited to the wedding feast (a

---

[25] Vernon Doerksen, "The Interpretation of Parables," *Grace Theological Journal* 11, no. 2 (1970): 17.

picture of the celebration of the kingdom coming to earth), and all they had to do was accept the invitation. The ones who refused to hear the messengers sent to them were punished because of their active rejection of the invitation given to them. It is the king who gets all the glory in providing the feast and the means to come to the feast, and those who reject the feast suffer his wrath for doing so.

Molinism says that both Calvinism and Arminianism are right with respect to salvation's requirement. Calvinism is correct that salvation is all of God; He is the one who does it all! Arminianism is also correct in saying that we are responsible not to resist the drawing of the Holy Spirit, and that the choice to reject the Spirit's work is possible. This is possible if faith is completely passive; if "trust" is not resisting what God calls us to and wants to do in us, then salvation can be completely of God while rejection of God is still completely our fault if it happens.

Sage Election[26]

The next question that arises in Molinism is how God's desires and our free will interact. If we have any role to play, then Calvinists will argue that God may well elect someone who chooses to reject Christ, leading to God's will being denied and Him not really being in charge. Arminians are concerned that if God sovereignly decides who is saved on His own, then choice is a lie and God is unloving and unjust to force a relationship upon us. Molinism says that because God is infinitely *sage* or "wise," He can choose who will be saved while preserving free will, offer the gospel to all, and not lose a single person who would have responded to the Gospel if they had heard it. That's a big God!

God can elect people to eternal life of His free will (much as Calvinism's *unconditional election*; see Romans 8:29-30) while not violating genuine human freedom of choice (much as Arminianism's *individual responsibility*; see Joshua 24:15). God has a genuine will for all to be saved and the Gospel is open to all. (1 Timothy 2:4; 2 Peter 3:9) At the same time, those who respond

---

[26] Keathley, *Salvation and Sovereignty*, 138–163.. Keathley calls this point "Sovereign Election," and he comes at it from a more Calvinist perspective than I do here. The term "sage" as an adjective means "wise, judicious" according to Catherine Soanes and Angus Stevenson, eds., *Concise Oxford English Dictionary: 11th Edition Revised 2008*, 11 Revised. (New York: Oxford University Press, USA, 2008). God's wisdom is what comes to the forefront in this point, and so I chose to use a term that means God uses His wisdom while preserving the acrostic ROSES. (ROWES is not so good.)

do so because God saved them all of Himself. (John 3:3-8; Ephesians 2:8-9) Those who do not respond to the Gospel are damned because of their free resistance to God. (Matthew 23:37) At the same time, God elected those who are saved before the foundation of the world. (Ephesians 1:4)

This is where God's Middle Knowledge really comes into sharp focus and is really necessary to understand. Does God elect, or do we choose to trust Christ and be saved? Though the battle ground between Calvinism and Arminianism is strewn with many fallen soldiers in this battle, the biblical answer to the debate is not to pick one or the other, but to answer *yes* to both. God elects, and our decision to trust Him is meaningful and free. Middle knowledge lets us do that while still recognizing the law of non-contradiction.[27]

Middle knowledge comes into play here because out of all of the possible worlds that God *could* have created, He chose to create the world in which all of His sovereign desires come to pass and does so in a way that violates no free decisions. All of those who

---

[27] If you're not familiar with this idea, my suggestion is to Google it. The Wikipedia article is good but geeky. If you're not so geeky, go to "Law of non-contradiction", n.d., http://carm.org/dictionary-law-of-non-contradiction. Online. (accessed June 22, 2012). In a nutshell, this law says that contradictory statements can't both be true in the same sense. Here's an example. If we say "Bill is human" and "Bill is not human," both of those statements can't be true in the same way. They contradict and therefore can't both be true.

come to Christ are those who are elect, and none of those who are lost would have come to faith in Christ in any other possible scenario. Thus both God's sovereignty and human responsibility are upheld.

This concept sounds complicated, but hang in there! Think of the world we actually live in as one of a mind-bogglingly large number of worlds that God could have possibly made. Out of the possible worlds, there is a smaller group of worlds where every one of those whom God has elected become Christians and are saved.[28] There is a different group of worlds out of all of the possible worlds where God allows people to have genuinely meaningful choices and free will. It is certainly within the realm of possibility that those different groups have some overlap. Where those possibilities overlap is where God in His wisdom actually chooses a world, in which all of those He has chosen (and only those He has chosen) come to faith in Christ, and do so because of genuinely free decisions. A diagram may help us visualize it.

---

[28] Maybe in some possible worlds, all people who are saved have blue eyes, or are left-handed, or can do one-arm pushups.

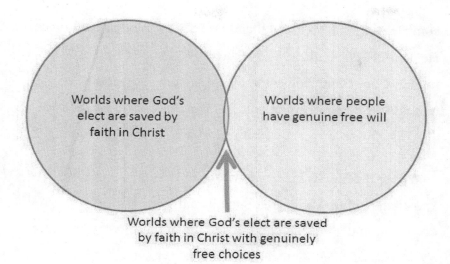

Worlds where God's
elect are saved by
faith in Christ

Worlds where people
have genuine free will

Worlds where God's elect are saved
by faith in Christ with genuinely
free choices

The size of the overlap is small in the diagram, but that's not the point. It may be that the overlap is huge, or they might actually just touch each other at one point[29] representing one possible world where God's will is carried out by free decisions. As long as there is at least one point of possibility, then God could choose to create this world where we have both free decisions and what He desires comes to pass.

God uses His infinite wisdom in Sage Election to bring about His perfect will while not violating freedom of choice for people. God could have created a world in which the elect come to faith in Christ because He forced them to. He could have created a world in which free will reigns and He elects someone but they don't

---

[29] All the math nerds just got excited and said "That's a tangent!"

come to faith in Christ and therefore they are never saved. Instead, He chose to create the world where all of the elect are saved by faith in Christ, and they come to Christ genuinely and freely. This upholds the sovereignty of God to create the world He chooses, and His choice to create us with free will at important moments.

God does this in His infinite wisdom and using His infinite knowledge of all of His creation, all of their possible free decisions, and all of the possible combinations of creation, people, and decisions in all their ridiculously large number of combinations. This is why Paul extols God's wisdom and knowledge in Romans 11:33-36:

> *"Oh, the depth of the riches and wisdom and knowledge of God! How unsearchable are his judgments and how inscrutable his ways! "For who has known the mind of the Lord, or who has been his counselor?" "Or who has given a gift to him that he might be repaid?" For from him and through him and to him are all things. To him be glory forever. Amen."*

In Romans 9-11 Paul discusses God's faithfulness to His promises, and how He accomplishes His intended ends while explaining human failure and our decisions to ignore Him or accept Him. At the end of this difficult discussion, Paul breaks forth in praise not to God's control or to our responsibility, but to God's *wisdom*[30] and *knowledge* at being in sovereign control while allowing His creatures to make meaningful choices. God knows all possibilities; more than that, though, God has perfect and infinite wisdom to choose the very best from the available possibilities without fail. He gets all the glory for His infinite wisdom in creating the world in which both His free and total control and our responsibility are not only possible but work together in perfect harmony!

God can create a world in which all of His elect come to faith in Christ, and ONLY His elect come to faith in Christ, and yet the decision to trust Christ or reject Him is a free and responsible decision for each person. His election is sage or wise, and He controls history using His wisdom rather than force or coercion or simple foreknowledge of what will come to pass. So *Sage Election* upholds the Calvinistic idea of God's sovereign control of history, because God is the One who decides which world to create out of the infinite number of possible worlds that He could have created. It also upholds the Arminian idea of individual responsibility, because according to Scripture the world that God actually chose

---

[30] If I wanted to stay with the theme of "Sage Election" I would have used the word "sagacity," but seriously when was the last time you heard that word?

to create is a world in which our decisions (at least at key moments like upon hearing the Gospel) are truly free.

Eternal Security[31]

While Calvinism holds to the Perseverance of the Saints (where all believers will persevere in a life of holiness until death), and Arminianism teaches Conditional Security (that believers are secure as long as they continue to believe), Molinism takes a tack that once again attempts to uphold parts of each while approaching the issue from a different perspective. Rather than think of the perseverance of the saints, Molinists prefer to talk about the *preservation* of the saints. We have eternal security not because of us in any way or anything within us, but because of the faithfulness of Jesus.

When we think of preservation, perhaps it is worthwhile to think of food. Most of the food that we buy in the store contains preservatives of one kind or another so that it stays edible for long enough for people to be able to eat it.[32] A fresh loaf of bread with

---

[31] Keathley, *Salvation and Sovereignty*, 164–190. Upon this point I will differ from Keathley in some respects. He takes a *genuine evidence* view of works, while coming very close to a classic Free Grace understanding of security of the saints. My explanation of this point will be along the lines of the Free Grace position, which he explains some and comes very close to. "Free Grace" theology as a system will be explained more in chapter 7.

[32] I can just feel someone reading this who is on a paleo diet or a strict organic eater reacting negatively that preservatives are bad. Okay, fine, I gotcha. Think

no preservatives (just flour, water, sugar, salt, and yeast) will last perhaps 2-3 days before molding or going stale, while a store-bought loaf with artificial preservatives might last weeks or even longer![33] The preservation keeps bread, which by itself would quickly spoil, edible. It's not something intrinsic to the bread itself that keeps it fresh, but something added from outside that keeps it edible.

This analogy (if not pushed too far) helps with our understanding of the security of our salvation too. If we were responsible for keeping our salvation, we would quickly lose it because we are still capable of significant sin, and still capable of renouncing Christ! (John 6:66) Likewise, we have a hard time using our works to showcase whether we are saved or not because it can give us false positives (Matthew 7:21-23) as well as false negatives. (John 12:42) We can still be pretty terrible sinners, even though we're sons and daughters of God! (Romans 7:14-25) Thankfully, it is nothing in us that keeps us secure; it is the faithfulness of Christ and the sealing of the Holy Spirit that act as the "preservative" to keep us from losing our salvation.

---

of it like a parable, and don't push the imagery too far! Preservatives preserve, which in the case of physical health might be less than perfect but in the case of spiritual life is a very good thing.
[33] We may lament the preservation of food in America where food is plentiful, but in much of the world where starvation is a real concern, preservation like this can save lives.

In Molinism, some important concepts from Calvinism and Arminianism are upheld, combined, and changed. Like Calvinism, Molinism believes that those who are truly born again can never lose their eternal life. (John 10:28)[34] Those who trust Christ for their eternal life can never be separated from His love for them in Christ. (Romans 8:38-39) Like Arminianism, Molinism can say that we continue to have significant free will even after we are saved, and that it is not certain that our faith will continue throughout life. True believers can shipwreck their faith! (1 Timothy 1:19)[35] There will be some who have trusted Christ for their eternal life who, at the end of their days, have nothing praiseworthy to show for their Christian walk. (1 Corinthians 3:15)

God preserves those who have trusted Christ even if they fail utterly and miserably. He does this not because there is anything good in them (obviously they've failed as Christians!), but because of His gracious goodness and mercy to His children. Because God preserves those who accept Christ, their security is far from conditional. Just as children need unconditional love from their

---

[34] This is not to say that everyone who *says* that they are a Christian really is. Matthew 7:21-23 tells us quite clearly that there will be some who call Jesus "Lord" at the end of days, and have done many good things in His name, who never trusted Him and Him alone for eternal life and will therefore spend eternity away from His presence. People also lie, so someone can say they trust Christ who really doesn't.

[35] Note that in order to "shipwreck their faith," someone must have faith that is their own to begin with. If it wasn't really faith, then they can't shipwreck their faith but some counterfeit.

parents, our Heavenly Father gives His children His love unconditionally. (2 Timothy 2:13) When God saves someone, that salvation should come with assurance of eternal life. (Hebrews 11:1; 2 Timothy 1:12)

Eternal life is guaranteed not on the basis of our own faithfulness but is instead founded upon the work of Jesus on behalf of believers on the cross. (Galatians 2:16[36]) It is not dependent upon our faithfulness to Jesus, thankfully, but upon His faithfulness to us! Thankfully, He doesn't make salvation depend on us being good and true to Him; we're not that great if we're really honest. God justifies or saves forever those who believe in Christ (John 3:16); He justifies the ungodly person, not just the person who becomes godly. (Romans 4:3-5)

This is not to say that God is okay with Christians going on sinning after they accept Christ; not at all! The Spirit will certainly sanctify His saints, but that sanctification may not show itself uniformly in the life of the saints or in a manner that we can verify from the outside all the time. As an example, both Abraham and Lot were

---

[36] On a geeky note, my understanding here takes its basis from a reading of Galatians 2:16 in the NET Bible that says, "…no one is justified by the works of the law but by the faithfulness of Jesus Christ…" Biblical Studies Press, *The NET Bible First Edition* (Richardson, TX: Biblical Studies Press, 2006). The argument for taking it that way can be found in Richard B. Hays, *The Faith of Jesus Christ: The Narrative Substructure of Galatians 3:1-4:11*, 2nd ed. (Grand Rapids, MI: Wm. B. Eerdmans Publishing Company, 2002).

saved according to 2 Peter 2:7-8, though their outward expression of being saved was radically different. Abraham walked with God, while Lot was not a very godly guy! John 12:42 says that even some among the authorities believed in Him[37], but didn't do a very good job of showing that because they were afraid. If a person has trusted Christ for eternal life, Christ in His faithfulness keeps them secure despite their worst failure. (Romans 8:38-39; 2 Tim 2:11-13)

It's also a misunderstanding of eternal security to say that God doesn't desire or demand our faithfulness; both the Old and New Testaments say over and over and over again that God wants and expects us to be holy. This is a significant command of God (1 Peter 1:15-16), and one that we are commanded to pursue. Jesus has some not so kind words for those who don't listen to Him and obey Him in Luke 6:46-49, and those words must ring in our ears.

God will evaluate each believer in Christ at the judgment seat of Christ. (Romans 14:10; 2 Corinthians 5:10) At that judgment, each person will be evaluated according to how they lived for Christ and built on the foundation of faith in Christ that they began with, as Paul says in 1 Corinthians 3:10-15:

---

[37] And note in John 1:12 and 3:16 and 20:31 this is the requirement to have eternal life, so these dudes are as saved as saved can be.

"According to the grace of God given to me, like a skilled master builder I laid a foundation, and someone else is building upon it. Let each one take care how he builds upon it. For no one can lay a foundation other than that which is laid, which is Jesus Christ. Now if anyone builds on the foundation with gold, silver, precious stones, wood, hay, straw— each one's work will become manifest, for the Day will disclose it, because it will be revealed by fire, and the fire will test what sort of work each one has done. If the work that anyone has built on the foundation survives, he will receive a reward. If anyone's work is burned up, he will suffer loss, though he himself will be saved, but only as through fire."

This passage shows that all who trust Christ are eternally secure, and that all who trust Christ will be evaluated for their faithfulness. All who trust Christ have the foundation identically laid by means of accepting Jesus; they cannot lay any other foundation according to v. 11. On the day that we appear before the judgment seat of Christ, we will be evaluated by Him. Here Paul uses a building analogy to discuss that evaluation; even more, he uses the analogy of fire! Jesus will put a torch to each one's work; the one who builds with lasting materials will receive a reward from Christ for all eternity, while the one who built with perishable materials will suffer loss. Note, though, in v. 15 that this person is still saved! They suffer loss and certainly will feel that keenly, but they do not lose their salvation. Even with no faithfulness to the commands of God to live a holy life, they are still accepted by God by faith alone.

Another passage that teaches us about our eternal security with significant responsibility is the Parable of the Minas in Luke 19:11-27.[38] In this passage there are really five different "actors": the master, three different servants (okay there are ten servants, but only three really play into the image of the parable), and the "citizens." The master goes away to receive a kingdom and gives his servants each a mina (worth about a quarter of a year's wages[39]). His citizens reject him, but his servants each receive a reward or rebuke based on how they use his mina. The citizens who reject the master are slain in his presence at the end of the parable.

The parable imagery is pretty easy to unpack: the master is Jesus, the citizens are those who reject Him (first Israel, then applicable to all who reject Him), and the servants represent those who accept

---

[38] Go get your Bible and read it. Now. Before you go any further in the paragraph. I mean it.

[39] Walter A. Elwell, ed., *Baker Encyclopedia of the Bible* (Grand Rapids, MI: Baker Pub Group, 1997), 2:2138.

Him. Even the servant who did nothing with his gift isn't slain like the rebellious citizens. Likewise, Jesus says that we are eternally secure at the moment of faith alone in Christ alone.

Molinism says that eternal life is just that: eternal. It has no end, and is secure in Christ because of His faithfulness rather than our own. It agrees with Calvinism that those who are born again can never lose their salvation while agreeing with Arminianism that true Christians can live in persistent sin and even, possibly, give up their faith in Christ. The difference is that Molinism says that eternal life is still given to these people, though a very vigorous understanding of accountability at the judgment seat of Christ still provides plenty of incentive to live for Christ in a faithful manner.

Singular Redemption[40]

The last petal of our ROSES is perhaps the least of a departure from the other flowers. In fact, some Calvinists[41] and most Arminians would probably agree with it. Functionally, it says that Jesus' death was enough for the sins of all people and the intent was to make salvation possible for all, though only those who trust Jesus actually experience the benefits of Jesus' sacrifice. We use the phrase *singular redemption* because while the death of Jesus is

---

[40] Keathley, *Salvation and Sovereignty*, 191–210.
[41] Driscoll, Mark, "Unlimited Limited Atonement", November 20, 2005, http://cdn.marshill.com/files/2005/11/20/20051120_unlimited-limited-atonement_document_9143.pdf. Online. (accessed June 23, 2012).

provided for all, the actual redemption of people occurs one at a time. It's a singular redemption because it applies to singular people, not to all people without distinction.

Christ's death is of sufficient value and of sufficient intent to pay for the sins of all people. It had infinite value, and God's intent was to make salvation available to all. (John 3:16) However, the benefits of the payment of Jesus are only applied and secured to us at our conversion. What this means is that God provided salvation for all (1 John 2:2) but those benefits are only applied to those who believe (John 10:15).[42] Though the death of Christ provides salvation for everyone without exception (1 Timothy 4:10), that salvation is only actually given to those who believe. (John 3:16) For those who reject Jesus, the atonement and actual, real provision of eternal life testifies against them at the Great White Throne judgment, where unbelievers will be judged and cast into the lake of fire. (John 3:18; Revelation 20:11-15)

It's helpful in distinguishing between the flowers at this point to see a distinction in the terms *provided*, *obtained*, and *secured*.[43] In Arminianism, the atonement *obtained* salvation for all but secured

---

[42] Keathley, *Salvation and Sovereignty*, 196. I am aware that there are some who believe in the idea of "universal propitiation," which means that Jesus' death not only *potentially* pays for the sins of all people but actually *does* pay for the sins of all people, meaning in fact that all people's sins are paid for. I don't believe that this does justice to Scripture in its entirety.

[43] Ibid., 193.

it for none. In Calvinism, salvation was actually *secured* for the elect but only for them; God only intended Christ's death to pay for the sins of believers. In Molinism, salvation was *provided* for all of humanity but applied only to those who believe.

What this understanding does is allows us to take several texts at face value. Jesus wants all people to come to Him, like 2 Peter 3:9 says, and that means that He died for them. He loves the world, the whole world including every person in it, so much that He died for them like John 3:16 teaches. At the same time, John 10:15 tells us that Jesus laid down His life specifically for the sheep, and in that instance He is speaking directly of the benefits of His sacrifice for them.

Perhaps the verse that speaks to this most clearly is 1 Timothy 4:10. It reads, *"For to this end we toil and strive, because we have our hope set on the living God, who is the Savior of all people, especially of those who believe."* God (in this case, God the Son, Jesus) is indeed the Savior of all people. There is no other Savior! (Acts 4:12) He died to pay for their sins. But He is *especially* the Savior of those who believe, for they alone experience the benefits of the Savior dying for them. In the end, then, the payment of Christ is unlimited in intent and extent, and limited in application. It is not either/or, it is both. This is why we refer to it as a Singular Redemption.

Strengths and Concerns of Molinism

We can keep the tenets of Molinism clear in our mind by remembering its flower, ROSES: **R**adical Depravity, **O**vercoming Grace, **S**age Election, **E**ternal Security, and **S**ingular Redemption. In many ways it plots a new course to understanding how God saves someone, trying to uphold many tenets of both Calvinism *and* Arminianism. For many, it is a refreshing grace! This is no mean feat, and in the process it has strengths and weaknesses like its predecessors.

Strengths:

+ It attempts to uphold both the true sovereignty of God and the responsibility of people, which Scripture affirms in various places.

+ Molinism doesn't have to qualify God's goodness in light of His glory or vice versa. It's able to uphold both. This is a significant advantage, because Scripture never paints God's attributes as being in conflict with one another or functioning in subordination to one another. His attributes are all eternally perfect and pure, and they work together well in Molinism.

+ In many places it is able to uphold the strongest points of both Calvinism and Arminianism, and by approaching the problems from a new perspective it shows that what we thought were contradictory priorities are actually able to be placed together without significant tension.

+ It gets to claim some of the strengths of Calvinism and some of the strengths of Arminianism. It can uphold genuine relationship like Arminians do, along with free will and human responsibility. Like Calvinism, it can uphold God's sovereignty and meticulous care for and control over creation.

Concerns:

- It rests upon a framework (Middle Knowledge) that is complicated and sometimes hard to understand. Explaining that God knows all possibilities in all possible worlds starts to sound like science fiction pretty quickly.

- It doesn't have a lot of popular support among prominent Evangelical Christian scholars. While Calvinists and Arminians abound in seminaries and Bible colleges around the world, finding Molinists takes more work. Though it is not "new" (the 12th century is hardly "new"), it has not caught the attention of a significant number of thinkers. Even so, there are a few notable scholars who have really embraced this system and showed its validity in philosophy and in Scripture: William Lane Craig, Alvin Plantinga, and Kenneth Keathley among several.

– We must consider whether free will is really and truly free if God ultimately decides which world to create. If He decides to create *this* world, in which decisions happen the way they do without fail, could we really have chosen otherwise? This is where the philosophers take over the discussion, and for many that discussion is too much like the discussion about how many angels can dance on the head of a pin.

If you'd like to read more about Molinism there are several books that will prove to be very helpful:

James K. Beilby and Paul R. Eddy, eds., *Divine Foreknowledge: Four Views* (Downers Grove, IL: IVP Academic, 2001). Multiview books are always helpful, and this one certainly is!

Colin Brown, *Christianity and Western Thought, Volume 1: From the Ancient World to the Age of Enlightenment* (Downers Grove, IL: IVP Academic, 2010). Pages 162-166 are particularly about the thinking of Luis de Molina.

William Lane Craig, *Divine Foreknowledge and Human Freedom: The Coherence of Theism: Omniscience* (Leiden:

Brill Academic Publishers, 2005). Be careful when approaching Craig. He is a deep thinker and this book is heavy sledding. Even so, it is really valuable reading.

_____, *The Only Wise God: The Compatibility of Divine Foreknowledge & Human Freedom* (Eugene, OR: Wipf & Stock Publishers, 2000)

Thomas P. Flint, *Divine Providence: The Molinist Account*, 1st ed. (Ithaca, NY: Cornell University Press, 2006).

Luis De Molina and Alfred J. Freddoso, *On Divine Foreknowledge: Part IV of the "Concordia" (Cornell Classics in Philosophy, "Concordia")* (Ithaca, NY: Cornell University Press, 2004). This is a translation of Molina's work with commentary from Freddoso, which is really helpful. In my opinion the system has advanced quite a ways in the past 800 years, but it's always helpful to get to the source of a view.

Kenneth Keathley, *Salvation and Sovereignty: A Molinist Approach* (Nashville, TN; B&H Academic, 2010). This is the book to start with for sure. It is readable and helpful and good for readers who don't have a degree in philosophy.

Alvin Plantinga, *God, Freedom, and Evil* (Grand Rapids, MI: William B. Eerdmans Publishing Company, 1978) Plantinga is an apologist and philosopher, and this book is a good approach to the problem of evil from a Molinist perspective.

Questions for Individual Thought and Group Discussion:

1. Which letter of ROSES do you think has the best evidence? Why is it strong?

2. Which letter of ROSES do you think has the most challenges? What are its weaknesses?

3. What do you think of Molinism's central idea of God's wisdom? Do you think that there is enough evidence in Scripture to make this the central idea of God in salvation?

4. Do you think that the idea of God's middle knowledge is supported in Scripture? Why or why not?

5. Eternal Life is the most controversial point of Molinism. Does it undermine the justice of God to save people if they turn away from Him? If eternal security does not depend on our perseverance, does our motivation for Christian living go away? Why or why not?

Chapter 6: Let's Get Planting!

It's now time to plant our garden, to decide which flowers we prefer to cultivate and care for. So which is it: TULIPs, LILACs, or ROSES? Each flower has strengths and weaknesses; each gives us a view of who God is and who we are as well as a system to understand how God's control and our free will interact in salvation. Each one tries to read the text of Scripture in a manner that does it justice, but each comes to the discussion with a different approach.

Some would rather not decide between them or plant any of them, but that approach has a lot of problems too. Trying to ignore the issue can lead to an inconsistent and contradictory set of beliefs in our life, and from those beliefs our mouths—and therefore our actions—spring. (Luke 6:45) In our flowerbox analogy, if we don't tend our flowerbox we end up with a garden full of weeds!

We could possibly pick and choose and plant a mixed box of flowers, and while that may sound appealing it has its share of problems. In the flower world, roses need a lot of water and lilacs won't bloom if they are watered too much; putting them in the same flowerbox means trouble, because what one needs the other can't have. Likewise, the different systems of understanding salvation have differing needs and priorities, and trying to take a piecemeal approach doesn't work in the long run while maintaining consistent biblical interpretation.

It's wise at this point to remember the wisdom we learned in chapter 4 about systems and their limits. At the end of the day we must pick the system whose problems we have the least problem with, whose issues are easiest for us to deal with, and whose benefits we like the best. Tulips can be finicky, lilacs are susceptible to disease, and roses have thorns, but each one gives us a pretty flower for the trouble of cultivating it! Their difficulties don't mean that we shouldn't plant them at all, but it does mean we need to consider the strengths and weaknesses of each as we look at planting our salvation garden. It means we should understand each one well, appreciate it for what it is worth, and choose to hold what we think has the most going for it while respecting those who differ with us and choose to plant their garden differently.

Calvinism highlights the greatness of God and His sovereign control over creation. Since God does all the work in bringing the elect to faith, we can rest knowing that no one will be lost because of our inability to evangelize well or because of our lack of initiative. God overcomes everything within us to bring us to faith, which makes salvation totally His. However, the challenges with Calvinism are significant. For many, God creating people purposefully knowing that He would send them to hell, solely for

His glory, seems far from good. Also, Calvinism brings a lack of assurance to many believers, knowing that some can experience temporary blessings and many signs of election and yet fail to persevere in the faith and therefore not be saved. Finally, the system does not seem to allow for honest relationship based on choosing to worship the Creator; forced relationship is no relationship.

Arminianism centers on the goodness of God and His desire to be in honest relationship with people. Those who trust Jesus do so of their own choice; God desires worship, not coerced service. He lovingly provides for that worship in prevenient grace. Because God's goodness is in sharp focus, His desire for all to be saved is a highlight of God's great mercy. Arminianism also stresses our individual responsibility and attempts to protect the justice of God by placing the blame for damnation at the feet of people rather than God. There are some significant challenges, though. Arminianism struggles with God's sovereignty and verses that seem to speak of His choice of people to be saved. It is difficult to see how we can be part of salvation without at least some of salvation being by our own merit. And assurance is still difficult to come by, because we can be saved today but leave the faith later and be lost.

Molinism brings the wisdom of God front and center and attempts to uphold both the goodness and greatness of God at the same time. God uses His middle knowledge to create a world where truly free decisions carry out His truly sovereign desires without denying either. God is truly sovereign and does all the work in salvation, while decisions are truly free and therefore meaningful in salvation. The greatest challenges facing Molinism are that it rests on God having middle knowledge which can be a bit complicated, and that it has not enjoyed the popularity that either Calvinism or Arminianism have.

At this point we also have to take stock of where we are: each system has some merits and some weaknesses. There is no avoiding that. So which do we adopt? Some Christians are dyed-in-the-wool Calvinists while others are thoroughly convinced Arminians. If you are one or the other, then hopefully this book is still valuable to you in helping to understand other viewpoints and building dialogue by means of that understanding. If nothing else, by following the rules set out in chapter 1 we at least make our discussions as Christians more encouraging and helpful! By all means, if TULIPs are your thing or LILACs are your flowers of choice, then at least take these chapters as a helpful introduction to alternate ways of solving the same dilemma you've faced.

For many of us, though, neither classical Calvinism nor classical Arminianism makes perfect sense because God is not primarily great or preeminently good, but is all of both and totally wise as well. If that is you, then maybe ROSES make better sense in your garden. If we can say that Scripture affirms that God is in control and all knowing, and yet also say that our decisions are truly meaningful, then Molinism allows us to see both of those as consequences of God's absolute wisdom in creating this world where both are possible. If it can be defended biblically, Molinism offers some significant advantages that combine the best of Calvinism and Arminianism to us in everyday life as well:

1. It gives us reliance on the sovereignty and control of God. He is always in control and we can rest in His care, knowing that He is all wise and nothing escapes His notice. He has the beginning, end, and middle in His hands. (Very Calvinist!)

2. It reminds us that our decisions are important and are our own. We are accountable for our decisions because they decide our fate. It is also helpful because we recognize that decisions we make today will limit our available choices later, meaning that our decisions have a snowball effect on our lives. (How Arminian!)

3. It shows us that we have a combination of unconditional love from God despite our worst failures and a strong motivation for godly living in our reception from Jesus into eternity as well as our eternal significance, not to mention

the motivation of gratitude to God for His work in our lives without merit on our part.

If Molinism makes the best sense of Scripture and is the most satisfying overall, we still have work to do. What does this understanding of the way people are saved mean for us in terms of practical living? Since theology affects life, what are the practical implications of adopting Molinism as our system for understanding God, people, and salvation? That is the task for our last chapter.[1]

Questions for Individual Thought and Group Discussion:

1. What was it about the system that you chose that causes you to think it is the best?

2. Have you honestly considered the real challenges with your system? What is the biggest "problem" with your system, and is the solution to the problem a good one?

3. What do you think are the biggest practical implications of your system? How does the "center" of your system affect everyday life?

---

[1] If you decided that Calvinism or Arminianism is the better approach, then I would encourage you to go get some of the books suggested in the chapters on those systems to put some feet to your faith and really think through the everyday issues it presents.

Chapter 7: ROSES in Full Bloom

So you've decided to plant ROSES. You've read the chapters, paged through Scripture and considered the verses, checked the pluses and minuses, compared them to TULIPs and LILACs and determined that ROSES are the best flowers to plant. The soil is all prepared, and the seeds are in the ground. But what kind of flower is going to come up? What will it look like, what will it smell like, and how will your garden bloom?

The final chapter looks at just that. If our theology has no practical impact on our life, then there is really no reason to talk about it. In reality, our theology *always* affects how we view life and how we act in the world; knowing that theology affects life as we adopt it is helpful because it allows us to match our actions to our beliefs purposefully and consciously rather than without thought. Molinism's ROSES affects the way we understand Scripture as well as impacts our walk with God, our outreach to others with the Gospel, and even affects the way we interact with the Calvinists and Arminians as well as others in our lives.

Interpreting Scripture

When we adopt a system or accept it as the best explanation of the evidence, it does impact the way we look at the biblical text.

Molinism is no different in this regard than any other. When we adopt the wisdom of God as the center of our understanding, and uphold both His sovereign control and our real freedom, it does affect the way we interpret Scripture.

This really comes to the front when looking at salvation passages. It allows us to come to passages that affirm God's control over salvation without qualifying them, and do the same when we come to passages affirming our responsibility. Neither qualifies or overrides the other, and God in His wisdom says that is the case. A great example of this is the hardening of Pharaoh's heart in the book of Exodus.[1] There is a lot of discussion about whether Pharaoh hardened his own heart or if God did it. Molinism answers that both are true, and both are affirmed in Scripture. God tells Pharaoh to let His people go, and Pharaoh resists the demands of God and brings destruction upon Himself. Where God is said to be the cause we accept that God was the cause. Where Pharaoh was said to be the cause, we uphold that Pharaoh actively resisted and that he had control over that decision. Where the Scripture is vague, we allow it to be vague and don't force the issue, knowing that it could be either.

---

[1] Find the references in Exodus 4:21, a whole bunch in chapters 7 through 10, 11:10, and 14:4, 8, and 17. More discussion on Pharaoh can be found in Anderson, *Free Grace Soteriology*, 286–288.

When we come to passages in Scripture that speak of the greatness and majesty of God, or passages speaking of His control over the world and knowledge of us and our ways, we can stand in awe of God and rejoice in that greatness. Likewise, when we come to passages upholding His absolute goodness and His desire for all people to be saved, we can rejoice in that goodness and affirm it at face value. This is perhaps the great advantage of Molinism, that each type of passage can be accepted with fewer qualifications or assumptions. This is a good thing!

Our walk with God

Our interpretation of Scripture builds our theology, and our theology leads us into our worship and walk with God. Right theology must always lead to right living![2] Since ROSES is a system of salvation, it should lead us in our understanding of how to live out our salvation as followers of Jesus. The implications for other areas of life (from economics, to church government, to politics, to marriage and parenting and more) are significant as well, but are beyond the scope of our study. Just focusing on the impact of Molinism on our walk with Christ from start to finish is enough to keep us occupied!

---

[2] Seminary students like the big words that *Orthodoxy* (correct worship) leads to *Orthopraxy* (right practice). The rule is, if you want your idea to sound important, say it in either Latin (preferably) or Greek.

Molinism affects every aspect of our walk with God, if we understand and apply it correctly. It affects how we understand becoming a Christian by faith in Christ (known as justification), how we grow more like Christ (i.e. sanctification), and how we will live forever in God's presence in eternity (glorification). In all of these, having God's wisdom at the center will be key (which makes sense, as this is the center of the whole system of Molinism). We must also remember that God is absolutely sovereign and that our decisions, especially at key moments, are important and meaningful. Molinism impacts the Christian walk in many ways. However, we will focus on some of the most significant impacts on the Christian life and confine our discussion to three ideas in each phase of the Christian life: justification, sanctification, and glorification.

Justification: Becoming a child of God

First, the decision to trust Jesus Christ for eternal life is truly free and meaningful. When Jesus says that "whoever believes in Him" will have eternal life, He means just that! (John 3:16) We must choose for ourselves to follow the Lord or not; it is our responsibility and one that God holds us accountable to. (Joshua 24:15) Because we have been given at least some free will by God, we are accountable for how we use that freedom. Nowhere is this truer than in the realm of our justification.

Second, though the responsibility is ours to use our free will, we get no credit and have no merit in our justification. That's because it's not really anything active in us that brings about our salvation. Remember, our part is to not resist the work of the Holy Spirit in our life. We are responsible to do nothing…literally! Any part that we have would bring merit to us and mean that salvation is not by grace alone and not by works, which it clearly is. (Ephesians 2:8-9) Therefore, we must never forget that though God holds us accountable for our decisions, the only decision in justification that we have is the decision to let God do everything to bring us to His kingdom. Faith, then, is completely passive and rests in God's work. This is cause to rejoice in the great work God does in us.

Third, salvation is truly by faith *alone* in Christ *alone*. God knows our heart, and works can be as much a false positive as they are a false negative. In Matthew 7:21-23, we see that there are plenty of people who will point to their great works as evidence that they knew God.[3] Jesus, though, says that He never knew them; their works did nothing to give eternal life and were not an indicator of whether the people who did them were saved. So we, too, can't look to works to say whether we are saved or not. Instead, we must

---

[3] Prophesying, casting out demons, and performing miracles all rank pretty high on the "awesome works of God" scale! These are probably just examples from Jesus' lips about the many ways at the end of time that people will attempt to justify themselves. In our world many more might say that they didn't cheat on their spouse, or they served in church, or they gave money to feed starving children in another country. None of that earns a thing with God.

look only and completely to Christ; the question is whether we have stopped trying to earn God's favor and instead looked completely to the work of Jesus for our eternal life. (Hebrews 4:10)

It's worth stopping for just a moment here to explain how this fits with James 2:14-26. Many scholars argue that James 2 says that if our faith doesn't work then it isn't real, but that's probably not the big lesson James was trying to convey[4]. First, let's realize that Paul was a HUGE proponent of salvation by faith alone in Christ alone; Romans 4:4-5, Galatians 2:16, and Ephesians 2:8-9 are evidence enough of that. Second, we must realize from Galatians 1:6-9 that Paul took this seriously and would never be friends with someone who taught that we are saved by works. In Galatians 2:7-10 Paul tells the Galatians that he and James were friends, which means that James agreed with Paul that before God, our justification is by faith alone in Christ alone. The problem is that in James 2:24 James explicitly says we are saved by works and not saved by faith alone. What gives?

The answer is that Paul and James are talking about different things. When Paul talks about justification he is talking about our acceptance before God. When James talks about justification he is talking about how other people view us and see our walk with

---

[4] The following discussion is more fully explained in Fred Chay and John P. Correia, *The Faith That Saves: The Nature of Faith in the New Testament* (Phoenix, AZ: Grace Line, Inc., 2008), 120–148.

God. We know this for several reasons. In James 2:14-17 James shows that his concern is practical; he has hungry people to feed, and just because someone is going to heaven doesn't mean they are any earthly good! Second, in verses 18 and 19 James introduces an accuser, someone who points out a potential flaw. Notice in these verses that the accuser is interested in showing other people his faith. God already knows, so there is no sense in showing Him! He asks another person to show them their faith, and he in turn will show them his faith. James also uses the examples of Abraham in verses 21-23 and Rahab in verse 25 to show that our works "justify" us not in God's eyes, but in the eyes of other people. They see our works and glorify God. For James, verse 24 says there is more than justification by faith (before God); there is also justification by works (before people).

As James 2:24 says, we are justified by works (to people) and not only justified by faith (to God). If we think about it, this practical focus of James is lived out in life all the time. We judge ourselves on our intent and desire; we want others to accept us because we tried or wanted their best. However, we accept others not based on their heart (which we can't see) but based on their actions (which we can). This is James' concern: how we relate to one another.

So salvation is 100% by faith alone in Christ alone. This is the message of the whole Bible. Jesus says it over and over in the

Gospel of John, Paul championed it throughout his letters, and his friend James merely reminds us that God sees our heart but people see our works. That's why we need to grow more like Christ and show them who He is!

Sanctification: Growing more like Christ

It is primary in our life with God to remember that He is all-wise, all-knowing, and completely in control. We can rest in the complete care of God, because not only is He in control, but He is completely good as well! This is where the combination of the best of Calvinism and Arminianism really pays off in Molinism. God is both great *and* good, and neither of those is qualified by the other. As we walk with Christ through the good times and the bad, we can rest in the sure conviction that whatever comes, Jesus will hold us firmly and lovingly in His hands. We can recite Psalm 23 with conviction and peace, knowing that even in the valley of the shadow of death our Shepherd looks over us. We can know that no matter how bad life might look God is good and that no matter how out of control life feels God is sovereign and wise.

Secondly, as we walk with God in the Christian life we must always remember that our decisions have consequences. We are responsible not to quench the Spirit (1 Thessalonians 5:19) or grieve the Spirit. (Ephesians 4:30) Jesus calls us to listen to Him and follow His directions, (Luke 6:46-49), and promises consequences either way. Because we have freedom of will we are accountable to God for our actions and for growing in Christ. We can never blame God for not progressing in the Christian life because the Scripture places that responsibility on our shoulders.

Third, we must realize that the work of growing more like Christ continues to be the work of God; our place is still not to resist. As we allow the Spirit to work within us, without our merit He transforms us to be more like Him and to become on the outside what we are on the inside. (Romans 8:12-17) It is submission to God that leads us into the blessings of God, and not our own merit. (James 4:7-10) He guides us and leads us into all truth. (John 14:26) Even when we grow in our faith and become more Christ-like, we must always remember that this is just what Christ redeemed us to do; there is no place for pride in the Christian life. (Luke 17:7-10)

Glorification: Forever in the presence of God

The first part of how Molinism affects our understanding of glorification is that Eternal life is just that: eternal. All those who have placed faith alone in Christ alone for their eternal life will spend eternity with God. (Revelation 20:11-15) God knew who those were before the world began, and He did not lose any who trusted Him. (John 10:28) All who have trusted Christ in this life will be with God forever, and this truth not only affects our glorification but also our sanctification. Because God guarantees our eternal life, we can rest knowing that His love for us is unconditional. (Romans 8:38-39) No failure on our part can possibly separate us from God's love, because even when Christians are faithless Jesus is faithful. (2 Timothy 2:13) God's unconditional love gives us great motivation and security as we seek to live for Him and still see ourselves sinning and failing in this world, because we know that no failure can cost us our eternal home with Jesus.

Molinism also gives us great motivation to serve Christ from His unconditional love because it recognizes the scrutiny and reward that we will each receive from Jesus in heaven. Christians will each stand before the Lord Jesus and give an account of what we did with the gift of eternal life that He gave us. The parable of the Minas in Luke 19:11-27 illustrates the difference between the servants who are each given a gift and the citizens who reject the king. Those who reject the king are a picture of unbelievers, but those who are given a gift are evaluated by the king for what they did with it and are a picture of believers.

This gets illustrated by Paul in 2 Corinthians 5:10, and especially 1 Corinthians 3:12-15. In these passages Paul says that we will all appear before the judgment seat of Christ to answer for how we used the gift of eternal life. In 1 Corinthians 3 we see that some build on the foundation of Christ with non-perishable materials and are rewarded for all time for that. Others instead build with perishable materials and suffer loss, though we must realize in verse 15 that Paul says that the person is still saved. Therefore glorification reminds us that we are loved unconditionally by God and also accountable to God for our life as Christians. This is powerful motivation for Christian living.

Spreading the Gospel of Jesus Christ

Molinism affects not only how we accept and live out the gospel but also impacts how we spread the gospel to others. In practical living and evangelism Molinism once again upholds the best of Calvinism and Arminianism in shaping the way we reach out to others with the message of redemption in Jesus. The first impact of Molinism is in tune with Arminianism, namely that the gospel message is truly open to all people. When we talk with someone, we can know that Jesus is the only savior they can possibly turn to and that He desires them to be saved. (2 Peter 3:9) He died to pay for their sins (1 John 2:2) and gives them the opportunity to trust Christ and become a child of God. (John 1:12) Jesus loves every human being, even with their sin, and wants them to worship Him in spirit and truth. The gospel message is truly good news!

The second impact of Molinism upon our evangelism is another Arminian strength, namely that decisions are significant and, especially with regard to accepting or rejecting Christ, are free decisions. There is no fatalism in our presentation because we cannot know the mind of God in the situation, but we can rest in faith knowing that God ensures that a person has a legitimate opportunity to accept the gospel. When we present someone with the gospel message, we can rest assured that the Holy Spirit is the one convicting them and making the gospel message understandable and real. In this sense, not only is their choice real but we can rest in the knowledge that it is not up to us to make the gospel clear, though of course we always strive to present the gospel clearly.

Third, God is in ultimate control and will lose no one who would possibly come to faith in Christ. This is a point most Calvinists would be delighted to affirm. God is the one who is in sovereign control of history, and He elects. (2 Thessalonians 2:13) Not only that, but He, in His wisdom, chose to create the world in which His election is carried out by completely free decisions! The upshot of this for us is that we can rest, knowing that God will never lose anyone who will come to faith in Christ. (John 10:28) Anyone who is lost, is lost because of their own rejection of Christ.

Finally, there is the issue of questionable cases. Sure, if someone hears the gospel message and rejects it that is one thing, but those who never hear of Christ, or die in infancy, or don't have the mental capacity to understand the gospel are a different case entirely. We must recognize that Scripture doesn't speak directly to the issue and that there is some mystery here for sure; to go beyond what is said by God is unwise. When we make absolute statements with no evidence we look foolish, and Scripture provides us with precious little evidence in these cases no matter how much we wish it weren't so.[5]

Perhaps, though, we can peer into the darkness a bit and get some idea. If Molinism is true, then we can say that God created the world in which truly free decisions carry out God's truly sovereign will. We can also say that God is absolutely wise, absolutely good, and absolutely sovereign. In His wise, good sovereignty God would never create a world in which someone is lost who would be saved under other circumstances. He knows all possibilities and what would happen if things had been otherwise. So therefore, the best that we can do is place these people in the hands of the God we know to be all wise, all good, and completely in charge and rest in the sure knowledge that He would never do anything unwise, unjust, and unloving with them since that would nullify His character. Exactly what that means for any given individual remains a mystery to us, but the character of God is no mystery.

---

[5] For more on this tough issue, I recommend Robert P. Lightner, *Safe in the Arms of Jesus: God's Provision for the Death of Those Who Cannot Believe* (Grand Rapids, MI: Kregel Publications, 2000).

Our Interaction with Calvinists and Arminians

Finally it is worth considering how Molinism gives us direction in our interactions with others over the issue of God's control and our free will. We must first and foremost realize that Molinism has limits as well. Nothing is perfect so we must be humble. We, like our brothers and sisters who are Calvinists and Arminians, are learning and growing and striving to be good thinkers who love God, love His word, and seek to live it out faithfully. We can accept in good faith that they are as well, and with a humble heart be willing to dialogue and grow together. We humbly admit that we are imperfect sinners who might be wrong. This spirit in dialogue with other Christians can move the discussion forward rather than keeping us locked in a battle of wills.

Secondly, there is much that we can affirm with our Calvinist and Arminian brothers and sisters in Christ. We have much common ground, even beyond the pillars of the faith we saw in chapter 1! We can have great fellowship with our Calvinist friends over the sovereignty of God, over His control and care of creation, and over His initiative in salvation. We can agree that salvation is all of God. Likewise, we can agree with our Arminian friends that (at least at critical junctures) we have free will. We can uphold with them that Christ died for the whole world and that God's grace is resistible. We can have healthy fellowship even when we don't agree 100%, because there is much that we do agree on. And even when we don't agree, we can recognize that each position is within the bounds of historic, orthodox Christianity and that we will see one another in heaven.

If you're interested in reading more on how to live the Christian life, especially with a Molinist view of salvation, there are many resources that can help you in that endeavor. Some of the better resources are:

Christian Living:

Charles C. Bing, *Living in the Family of Grace: A Workbook for Disciples* (Burleson, TX: GraceLife Ministries, 2003). This is a workbook that new Christians should work through with a mentor when they become a believer. It gives a wonderful foundation for Christian living.

Kenneth Boa, *Conformed to His Image: Biblical and Practical Approaches to Spiritual Formation* (Grand Rapids, MI: Zondervan, 2001). After using the previous book, this one is really helpful to work on growing in Christ.

Theology:

David R. Anderson, *Free Grace Soteriology* (n.p.: Xulon Press, 2010). This is a good introduction to salvation from a Free Grace perspective.

Joseph C. Dillow, *The Reign of the Servant Kings: A Study of Eternal Security and the Final Signficance of Man*, 2nd ed. (Haysville, NC: Schoettle Pub Co, 1992). Dillow's work is a great exposition of Hebrews and the gospel message.

C. Gordon Olson, *Getting the Gospel Right: A Balanced View of Calvinism and Arminianism* (Cedar Knolls, NJ: Global Gospel Publishers, 2005). While not really Molinist in a classical sense, Olson makes difficult issues easy to understand.

Mark Spencer, *A Moment In Time: Issues That Enhance Spiritual Multiplication* (Bloomington, IN: WestBowPress, 2012). This is an introduction to Free Grace theology that is readable and helpful for people new to Free Grace theology.

Politics:

James Davison Hunter, *To Change the World: The Irony, Tragedy, and Possibility of Christianity in the Late Modern World* (New York: Oxford University Press, USA, 2010). The value of this book is that it does not argue for either the political left or right, but critiques both and offers an alternative to political activism for Christians.

Ethics:

Norman L. Geisler, *Christian Ethics: Contemporary Issues and Options*, 2nd ed. (Grand Rapids, MI: Baker Academic, 2010). This is a revised and greatly expanded edition of a classic work on ethics, and is good reading.

Dennis P. Hollinger, *Choosing the Good: Christian Ethics in a Complex World* (Grand Rapids, MI: Baker Academic, 2002).

Questions for Individual Thought and Group Discussion:
1. What is your motivation for living a godly life? Has this discussion of our walk with God changed your idea of why we live for Jesus?

2. Does a combination of unconditional security and evaluation by Jesus provide a healthy spiritual motivation to serve the Lord? Why or why not?

3. What is hardest issue for you about evangelism? Does understanding our responsibility and God's control make it

easier for you to share the good news of Jesus with others? Why or why not?

4. If we admit that our system could be wrong and that we see value in others' systems, does that devalue our ability to dialogue with them or does it enhance it? What benefits can come in this discussion if we adopt this approach? What are the dangers?

Chapter 8: Flowers and Theology, Some Final Thoughts

We've realized that we have a flower box that needs planting. We've considered the flowers with their strengths and concerns, and made some honest appraisals of each. We've thought about the limits of systems and how to make sure not to overstep the bounds. We've finally decided that ROSES best represent all of Scripture and planted them, then watched the shoots turn into plants with beautiful bulbs. Congratulations! You're a theological horticulturalist!

As you go from here, realize that this book is just the tip of the iceberg; this is a beginning botany class, not a master's degree in horticulture. I applaud you for wanting to know more and for spending time studying theology and I encourage you to do some more of this kind of research. If you're burned out on systems and salvation, take up another interest in Christian doctrine and get some information by reading and listening and talking with others. Maybe your next topic is men and women in ministry, or spiritual gifts, or the connection between the church and Israel. Whatever it is, realize that you have the capacity to be informed on that issue as well.

Please, though, don't take this book as the end of your study of salvation. I hope by this point that your copy is dog-eared, highlighted, marked up in pencil, and has lots of Scripture circled. I hope you looked the verses up and considered them in their context. Please keep that attitude and keep studying, and always remain humble and ready to learn and grow and change. Never lose the heart of a noble Berean from Acts 17:11!

If at the end of this you're a Molinist (as I am), then you know that God is sovereign and in control, and that your decisions matter. So use that wonderful free will, under the sovereignty of God, and put this knowledge to work in your life. Remember that "'knowledge' puffs up, but love builds up." (1 Corinthians 8:1) Use it to love others and help them grow in their understanding of and walk with Christ.

If you're a Calvinist or an Arminian, I love the dialogue and invite it. My heart is that at least you've grown in your understanding of the various options and that this book has challenged you to know what you believe and why. If it has, then may God bless you as you serve Him with deeper commitment and determination.

Scripture Index

Works Cited

Adler, Mortimer J., and Charles Van Doren. *How to Read a Book: The Classic Guide to Intelligent Reading*. New York: Simon & Schuster, 1972.

Allen, David L., and Steve W. Lemke, eds. *Whosoever Will: A Biblical-Theological Critique of Five-Point Calvinism*. Nashville, TN: B&H Academic, 2010.

Anderson, David R. *Free Grace Soteriology*. n.p.: Xulon Press, 2010.

Aristotle. *Aristotle in 23 Volumes*. Translated by Hugh Tredennick. Vol. 17, 18. Cambridge, MA: Harvard University Press, 1933.

Beilby, James K., and Paul R. Eddy, eds. *Divine Foreknowledge: Four Views*. Downers Grove, IL: IVP Academic, 2001.

Biblical Studies Press. *The NET Bible First Edition*. Richardson, TX: Biblical Studies Press, 2006.

Bing, Charles C. *Living in the Family of Grace: A Workbook for Disciples*. Burleson, TX: GraceLife Ministries, 2003.

Boa, Kenneth. *Conformed to His Image: Biblical and Practical Approaches to Spiritual Formation*. Grand Rapids, MI: Zondervan, 2001.

Brown, Colin. *Christianity and Western Thought, Volume 1: From the Ancient World to the Age of Enlightenment*. Downers Grove, IL: IVP Academic, 2010.

Calvin, John. *Institutes of the Christian Religion*. Revised. Hendrickson Publishers, Inc., 2007.

Chay, Fred, and Correia, John P. *The Faith That Saves: The Nature of Faith in the New Testament*. Phoenix, AZ: Grace Line, Inc., 2008.

Craig, William Lane. *Brill's Studies in Intellectual History, Divine Foreknowledge and Human Freedom: The Coherence of Theism: Omniscience*. Leiden: Brill Academic Publishers, 2005.

————. *The Only Wise God: The Compatibility of Divine Foreknowledge & Human Freedom*. Eugene, OR: Wipf & Stock Publishers, 2000.

Dillow, Joseph C. *The Reign of the Servant Kings: A Study of Eternal Security and the Final Signficance of Man*. 2nd ed. Haysville, NC: Schoettle Pub Co, 1992.

Driscoll, Mark, and Gerry Breshears. *Doctrine (Paperback Edition): What Christians Should Believe*. Wheaton, IL: Crossway, 2011.

Driscoll, Mark. "Unlimited Limited Atonement", November 20, 2005. http://cdn.marshill.com/files/2005/11/20/20051120_unlimit ed-limited-atonement_document_9143.pdf (accessed June 23, 2012).

Earls, Aaron. "Theological Flower Bed: TULIP, DAISY & ROSES." *The Wardrobe Door*, August 2, 2010. http://wardrobedoor.blogspot.com/2010/08/theological-flower-bed-tulip-daisy.html (accessed June 13, 2012).

Ellis, John. *Eye-Deep in Hell: Trench Warfare in World War I*. Baltimore, MD: The Johns Hopkins University Press, 1989.

Elwell, Walter A., ed. *Baker Encyclopedia of the Bible*. Grand Rapids, MI: Baker Pub Group, 1997.

Flint, Thomas P. *Divine Providence: The Molinist Account*. 1st ed. Ithaca, NY: Cornell University Press, 2006.

Forell, George W. *Luther's Works, Volume 32: Career of the Reformer II*. Edited by Helmut T. Lehman. Minneapolis: Fortress Press, 1958.

Forlines, F. Leroy. *Classical Arminianism*. Edited by J. Matthew Pinson. Randall House Publications, 2011.

Geisler, Norman L. *Chosen But Free: A Balanced View of God's Sovereignty and Free Will*. 3rd ed. Minneapolis, MN: Bethany House Publishers, 2010.

————. *Christian Ethics: Contemporary Issues and Options*. 2nd ed. Grand Rapids, MI: Baker Academic, 2010.

Grenz, Stanley J., David Guretzki, and Cherith Fee Nordling. *Pocket Dictionary of Theological Terms*. Downers Grove, IL: IVP Academic, 1999.

Grudem, Wayne. *Systematic Theology: An Introduction to Biblical Doctrine*. Zondervan, 1994.

Harrison, A. W. *The beginnings of Arminianism to the Synod of Dort,*. First ed. University of London press, 1926.

Hays, Richard B. *The Faith of Jesus Christ: The Narrative Substructure of Galatians 3:1-4:11*. 2nd ed. Grand Rapids, MI: Wm. B. Eerdmans Publishing Company, 2002.

Hollinger, Dennis P. *Choosing the Good: Christian Ethics in a Complex World*. Grand Rapids, MI: Baker Academic, 2002.

Horton, Michael S. *For Calvinism*. Grand Rapids, MI: Zondervan, 2011.

Hunt, Dave, and James White. *Debating Calvinism: Five Points, Two Views*. Multnomah Books, 2004.

Hunter, James Davison. *To Change the World: The Irony, Tragedy, and Possibility of Christianity in the Late Modern World*. New York: Oxford University Press, USA, 2010.

Keathley, Kenneth. *Salvation and Sovereignty: A Molinist Approach*. B&H Academic, 2010.

Kendall, R. T. *Calvin and English Calvinism to 1649*. Wipf & Stock Publishers, 2011.

Larrimore, Mark. *The Problem of Evil: A Reader*. 1st ed. Hoboken, NJ: Wiley-Blackwell, 2000.

Lightner, Robert P. *Safe in the Arms of Jesus: God's Provision for the Death of Those Who Cannot Believe*. Grand Rapids, MI: Kregel Publications, 2000.

Mark Ross. "In Essentials Unity, In Non-Essentials Liberty, In All Things Charity." *Ligonier.org*, September 1, 2009. http://www.ligonier.org/learn/articles/essentials-unity-non-essentials-liberty-all-things/ (accessed July 4, 2012).

Marshall, I. Howard. *New Testament Theology: Many Witnesses, One Gospel*. Downers Grove, IL: IVP Academic, 2004.

Molina, Luis De, and Alfred J. Freddoso. *On Divine Foreknowledge: Part IV of the "Concordia" (Cornell Classics in Philosophy, "Concordia")*. Ithaca, NY: Cornell University Press, 2004.

Olson, C. Gordon. *Getting the Gospel Right: A Balanced View of Calvinism and Arminianism*. Cedar Knolls, NJ: Global Gospel Publishers, 2005.

Olson, Roger E. *Against Calvinism*. Grand Rapids, MI: Zondervan, 2011.

———. *Arminian Theology: Myths and Realities*. Fifth Printing. Downers Grove, IL: IVP Academic, 2006.

Peterson, Robert A., and Michael D. Williams. *Why I Am Not an Arminian*. IVP Books, 2004.

Peterson, Susan L., Hannah, John D., and Holden, Joseph. *Timeline Charts of the Western Church*. Grand Rapids, MI: Zondervan, 1999.

Picirilli, Robert E. *Grace, Faith, Free Will*. Randall House Publications, 2002.

Pinson, J. Matthew, ed. *Four Views on Eternal Security*. Grand Rapids, MI: Zondervan, 2002.

Piper, John. *The Justification of God: An Exegetical and Theological Study of Romans 9:1-23*. 2nd ed. Grand Rapids, MI: Baker Academic, 1993.

Plantinga, Alvin. *God, Freedom, and Evil*. Grand Rapids, MI: William B. Eerdmans Publishing Company, 1978.

Soanes, Catherine, and Angus Stevenson, eds. *Concise Oxford English Dictionary: 11th Edition Revised 2008*. 11 Revised. New York: Oxford University Press, USA, 2008.

Spencer, Mark. *A Moment In Time: Issues That Enhance Spiritual Multiplication*. Bloomington, IN: WestBowPress, 2012.

Sproul, R. C. *Chosen by God*. Carol Stream, IL: Tyndale House Publishers, Inc., 1994.

———. *What is Reformed Theology?: Understanding the Basics*. Baker Books, 2005.

Steele, David N., Curtis C. Thomas, and S. Lance Quinn. *Five Points of Calvinism, The: Defined, Defended, and*

Documented. 2nd ed. Phillipsburg, NJ: P & R Publishing, 2004.

Storms, Sam. *Chosen for Life: The Case for Divine Election*. Wheaton, IL: Crossway, 2007.

Vernon Doerksen. "The Interpretation of Parables." *Grace Theological Journal* 11, no. 2 (1970): 3–20.

Version, English Standard. *The Holy Bible: English Standard Version*. Downers Grove, IL: Crossway, 2006.

Walls, Jerry L., and Joseph R. Dongell. *Why I Am Not a Calvinist*. IVP Books, 2004.

Ware, Bruce A. *God's Lesser Glory: The Diminished God of Open Theism*. Downers Grove, IL: Crossway, 2000.

Wikipedia contributors. "Rafflesia." *Wikipedia, the free encyclopedia*. Wikimedia Foundation, Inc., June 12, 2012. http://en.wikipedia.org/w/index.php?title=Rafflesia&oldid= 496980333 (accessed June 15, 2012).

"Denouement: Aristotle and accuracy." *Denouement*, February 22, 2009. http://publicnoises.blogspot.com/2009/02/aristotle-and-accuracy.html (accessed June 12, 2012).

"Law of non-contradiction", n.d. http://carm.org/dictionary-law-of-non-contradiction (accessed June 22, 2012).

"The Canons of Dordt", n.d. http://www.reformed.org/documents/index.html?mainfram e=http://www.reformed.org/documents/canons_of_dordt.ht ml (accessed June 12, 2012).

"The Chicago Statement on Biblical Inerrancy". International Council on Biblical Inerrancy, 1978. http://library.dts.edu/Pages/TL/Special/ICBI_1.pdf (accessed June 21, 2012).